MASTER THE™ DSST®

Personal Finance Exam

About Peterson's

Peterson's has been your trusted educational publisher for over 50 years. It's a milestone we're quite proud of, as we continue to offer the most accurate, dependable, high-quality educational content in the field, providing you with everything you need to succeed. No matter where you are on your academic or professional path, you can rely on Peterson's for its books, online information, expert test-prep tools, the most up-to-date education exploration data, and the highest quality career success resources—everything you need to achieve your education goals. For our complete line of products, visit **www.petersons.com.**

For more information, contact Peterson's, 4380 S. Syracuse St., Suite 200, Denver, CO 80237; 800-338-3282 Ext. 54229; or visit us online at **www.petersons.com.**

ISBN-13: 978-0-7689-4466-2

Printed in the United States of America

10 9 8 7 6 5 4 3 2 1   23 22 21

Contents

Before You Begin

HOW THIS BOOK IS ORGANIZED

Peterson's *Master the*™ *DSST® Personal Finance* provides a diagnostic test, subject-matter review, and a post-test.

- **Diagnostic Test**—Twenty multiple-choice questions, followed by an answer key with detailed answer explanations
- **Assessment Grid**—A chart designed to help you identify areas that you need to focus on based on your test results
- **Subject-Matter Review**—General overview of the exam subject, followed by a review of the relevant topics and terminology covered on the exam
- **Post-test**—Sixty multiple-choice questions, followed by an answer key and detailed answer explanations

The purpose of the diagnostic test is to help you figure out what you know—or don't know. The twenty multiple-choice questions are similar to the ones found on the DSST exam, and they should provide you with a good idea of what to expect. Once you take the diagnostic test, check your answers to see how you did. Included with each correct answer is a brief explanation regarding why a specific answer is correct, and in many cases, why other options are incorrect. Use the assessment grid to identify the questions you miss so that you can spend more time reviewing that information later. As with any exam, knowing your weak spots greatly improves your chances of success.

Following the diagnostic test is a subject-matter review. The review summarizes the various topics covered on the DSST exam. Key terms are defined; important concepts are explained; and when appropriate, examples are provided. As you read the review, some of the information may seem familiar while other information may seem foreign. Again, take note of the unfamiliar because that will most likely cause you problems on the actual exam.

After studying the subject-matter review, you should be ready for the post-test. The post-test contains sixty multiple-choice items, and it will serve as a dry run for the real DSST exam. There are complete answer explanations at the end of the test.

OTHER DSST® PRODUCTS BY PETERSON'S

Books, flashcards, practice tests, and videos available online at **www.petersons.com/testprep/dsst**

- A History of the Vietnam War
- Art of the Western World
- Astronomy
- Business Mathematics
- Business Ethics and Society
- Civil War and Reconstruction
- Computing and Information Technology
- Criminal Justice
- Environmental Science
- Ethics in America
- Ethics in Technology
- Foundations of Education
- Fundamentals of College Algebra
- Fundamentals of Counseling
- Fundamentals of Cybersecurity
- General Anthropology
- Health and Human Development
- History of the Soviet Union
- Human Resource Management

- Introduction to Business
- Introduction to Geography
- Introduction to Geology
- Introduction to Law Enforcement
- Introduction to World Religions
- Lifespan Developmental Psychology
- Math for Liberal Arts
- Management Information Systems
- Money and Banking
- Organizational Behavior
- Personal Finance
- Principles of Advanced English Composition
- Principles of Finance
- Principles of Public Speaking
- Principles of Statistics
- Principles of Supervision
- Substance Abuse
- Technical Writing

Like what you see? Get unlimited access to Peterson's full catalog of DSST practice tests, instructional videos, flashcards, and more for **75% off the first month!** Go to **www.petersons.com/testprep/dsst** and use coupon code **DSST2020** at checkout. Offer expires July 1, 2021.

Chapter 1

All About the DSST® Exam

WHAT IS DSST®?

Previously known as the DANTES Subject Standardized Tests, the DSST program provides the opportunity for individuals to earn college credit for what they have learned outside of the traditional classroom. Accepted or administered at more than 1,900 colleges and universities nationwide and approved by the American Council on Education (ACE), the DSST program enables individuals to use the knowledge they have acquired outside the classroom to accomplish their educational and professional goals.

WHY TAKE A DSST® EXAM?

DSST exams offer a way for you to save both time and money in your quest for a college education. Why enroll in a college course in a subject you already understand? For more than 30 years, the DSST program has offered the perfect solution for individuals who are knowledgeable in a specific subject and want to save both time and money. A passing score on a DSST exam provides physical evidence to universities of proficiency in a specific subject. More than 1,900 accredited and respected colleges and universities across the nation award undergraduate credit for passing scores on DSST exams. With the DSST program, individuals can shave months off the time it takes to earn a degree.

The DSST program offers numerous advantages for individuals in all stages of their educational development:

- Adult learners
- College students
- Military personnel

Adult learners desiring college degrees face unique circumstances—demanding work schedules, family responsibilities, and tight budgets. Yet adult learners also have years of valuable work experience that can be applied toward a degree through the DSST program. For example, adult learners with on-the-job experience in business and management might be able to skip the Business 101 courses if they earn passing marks on DSST exams such as Introduction to Business and Principles of Supervision.

Adult learners can put their prior learning into action and move forward with more advanced course work. Adults who have never enrolled in a college course may feel a little uncertain about their abilities. If this describes your situation, then sign up for a DSST exam and see how you do. A passing score may be the boost you need to realize your dream of earning a degree. With family and work commitments, adult learners often feel they lack the time to attend college. The DSST program provides adult learners with the unique opportunity to work toward college degrees without the time constraints of semester-long course work. DSST exams take two hours or less to complete. In one weekend, you could earn credit for multiple college courses.

The DSST exams also benefit students who are already enrolled in a college or university. With college tuition costs on the rise, most students face financial challenges. The fee for each DSST exam starts at $85 (plus administration fees charged by some testing facilities)—significantly less than the $750 average cost of a 3-hour college class. Maximize tuition assistance by taking DSST exams for introductory or mandatory course work. Once you earn a passing score on a DSST exam, you are free to move on to higher-level course work in that subject matter, take desired electives, or focus on courses in a chosen major.

Not only do college students and adult learners profit from DSST exams, but military personnel reap the benefits as well. If you are a member of the armed services at home or abroad, you can initiate your post-military career by taking DSST exams in areas with which you have experience. Military personnel can gain credit anywhere in the world, thanks to the fact that almost all of the tests are available through the internet at designated testing locations. DSST testing facilities are located at more than 500 military installations, so service members on active duty can get a jump-start on a post-military career with the DSST program. As an additional incentive, DANTES (Defense Activity for Non-Traditional Education Support) provides funding for DSST test fees for eligible members of the military.

More than 30 subject-matter tests are available in the fields of Business, Humanities, Math, Physical Science, Social Sciences, and Technology.

Available DSST® Exams

Business	Social Sciences
Business Ethics and Society	A History of the Vietnam War
Business Mathematics	Art of the Western World
Computing and Information Technology	Criminal Justice
Human Resource Management	Foundations of Education
Introduction to Business	Fundamentals of Counseling
Management Information Systems	General Anthropology
Money and Banking	History of the Soviet Union
Organizational Behavior	Introduction to Geography
Personal Finance	Introduction to Law Enforcement
Principles of Finance	Lifespan Developmental Psychology
Principles of Supervision	Substance Abuse
	The Civil War and Reconstruction

Humanities	Physical Sciences
Ethics in America	Astronomy
Introduction to World Religions	Environment Science
Principles of Advanced English	Health and Human Development
Composition	Introduction to Geology
Principles of Public Speaking	

Math	Technology
Fundamentals of College Algebra	Ethics in Technology
Math for Liberal Arts	Fundamentals of Cybersecurity
Principles of Statistics	Technical Writing

As you can see from the table, the DSST program covers a wide variety of subjects. However, it is important to ask two questions before registering for a DSST exam.

1. Which universities or colleges award credit for passing DSST exams?
2. Which DSST exams are the most relevant to my desired degree and my experience?

Knowing which universities offer DSST credit is important. In all likelihood, a college in your area awards credit for DSST exams, but find out before taking an exam by contacting the university directly. Then review the list of DSST exams to determine which ones are most relevant to the degree you are seeking and to your base of knowledge. Schedule an appointment with your college adviser to determine which exams best fit your degree program and which college courses the DSST exams can replace. Advisers should also be able to tell you the minimum score required on the DSST exam to receive university credit.

DSST® TEST CENTERS

You can find DSST testing locations in community colleges and universities across the country. Check the DSST website (**www.getcollegecredit.com**) for a location near you or contact your local college or university to find out if the school administers DSST exams. Keep in mind that some universities and colleges administer DSST exams only to enrolled students. DSST testing is available to men and women in the armed services at more than 500 military installations around the world.

HOW TO REGISTER FOR A DSST® EXAM

Once you have located a nearby DSST testing facility, you need to contact the testing center to find out the exam administration schedule. Many centers are set up to administer tests via the internet, while others use printed materials. Almost all DSST exams are available as online tests, but the method used depends on the testing center. The cost for each DSST exam starts at $85, and many testing locations charge a fee to cover their costs for administering the tests. Credit cards are the only accepted payment method for taking online DSST exams. Credit card, certified check, and money order are acceptable payment methods for paper-and-pencil tests.

Test takers are allotted two score reports—one mailed to them and another mailed to a designated college or university, if requested. Online tests generate unofficial scores at the end of the test session, while individuals taking paper tests must wait four to six weeks for score reports.

PREPARING FOR A DSST® EXAM

Even though you are knowledgeable in a certain subject matter, you should still prepare for the test to ensure you achieve the highest score possible. The first step in studying for a DSST exam is to find out what will be on the specific test you have chosen. Information regarding test content is located on the DSST fact sheets, which can be downloaded at no cost from **www.getcollegecredit.com**. Each fact sheet outlines the topics covered on a subject-matter test, as well as the approximate percentage assigned to each topic. For example, questions on the Personal Finance exam are distributed in the following way: Foundations of Business—10%, Credit and Debt—15%, Major Purchases—15%, Taxes—15%, Insurance—15%, Investments—15%, and Retirement and Estate Planning—15%.

In addition to the breakdown of topics on a DSST exam, the fact sheet also lists recommended reference materials. If you do not own the recommended books, then check college bookstores. Avoid paying high prices for new textbooks by looking online for used textbooks. Don't panic if you are unable to locate a specific textbook listed on the fact sheet; the textbooks are merely recommendations. Instead, search for comparable books used in university courses on the specific subject. Current editions are ideal, and it is a good idea to use at least two references when studying for a DSST exam. Of course, the subject matter provided in this book will be a sufficient review for most test takers. However, if you need additional information, then it is a good idea to have some of the reference materials at your disposal when preparing for a DSST exam.

Fact sheets include other useful information in addition to a list of reference materials and topics. Each fact sheet includes subject-specific sample questions like those you will encounter on the DSST exam. The sample questions provide an idea of the types of questions you can expect on the exam. Test questions are multiple-choice with one correct answer and three incorrect choices.

The fact sheet also includes information about the number of credit hours ACE has recommended be awarded by colleges for a passing DSST exam score. However, you should keep in mind that not all universities and colleges adhere to the ACE recommendation for DSST credit hours. Some institutions require DSST exam scores higher than the minimum score recommended by ACE. Once you have acquired appropriate reference materials and you have the outline provided on the fact sheet, you are ready to start studying, which is where this book can help.

TEST DAY

After reviewing the material and taking practice tests, you are finally ready to take your DSST exam. Follow these tips for a successful test day experience.

1. **Arrive on time.** Not only is it courteous to arrive on time to the DSST testing facility, but it also allows plenty of time for you to take care of check-in procedures and settle into your surroundings.
2. **Bring identification.** DSST test facilities require that candidates bring a valid government-issued identification card with a current photo and signature. Acceptable forms of identification include a current driver's license, passport, military identification card, or state-issued identification card. Individuals who fail to bring proper identification to the DSST testing facility will not be allowed to take an exam.
3. **Bring the right supplies.** If your exam requires the use of a calculator, you may bring a calculator that meets the specifications. For paper-based exams, you may also bring No. 2 pencils with an eraser and black ballpoint pens. Regardless of the exam methodology, you are NOT allowed to bring reference or study materials, scratch paper, or electronics such as cell phones, personal handheld devices, cameras, alarm wrist watches, or tape recorders to the testing center.
4. **Take the test.** During the exam, take the time to read each question-and-answer option carefully. Eliminate the choices you know are incorrect to narrow the number of potential answers. If a question completely stumps you, take an educated guess and move on—remember that DSSTs are timed; you will have 2 hours to take the exam.

With the proper preparation, DSST exams will save you both time and money. So join the thousands of people who have already reaped the benefits of DSST exams and move closer than ever to your college degree.

PERSONAL FINANCE EXAM FACTS

The DSST® Personal Finance exam consists of 100 multiple-choice questions that cover debit and credit, major purchases, taxes, insurance, investments, and retirement and estate planning. Careful reading, critical thinking, and logical analysis will be as important as your knowledge of finance-related topics.

Area or Course Equivalent: Personal Finance
Level: Lower-level baccalaureate
Amount of Credit: 3 Semester Hours
Minimum Score: 400
Source: https://www.getcollegecredit.com/wp-content/assets/
factsheets/PersonalFinance.pdf

I. **Foundations of Business – 10%**

   a. Financial goals and values

   b. Budgeting and financial statements

   c. Cash management

   d. Economic terminology

   e. Institutional aspects of financial planning

II. **Credit and Debt – 15%**

   a. Credit and debit cards

   b. Installment loans

   c. Interest calculations

   d. Federal credit laws

   e. Creditworthiness, credit scoring, and reporting

   f. Bankruptcy

III. **Major Purchases – 15%**

   a. Auto, furniture, appliances

   b. Housing

IV. **Taxes – 15%**

   a. Payroll

   b. Income

   c. IRS and audits

   d. Estate and gift

   e. Tax planning/estimating

   f. Progressive vs. regressive

   g. Other (excise, property, sales, gas)

   h. Tax professionals

V. Insurance – 15%

a. Risk management

b. Life policies

c. Property and liability policies

d. Health, disability, and long-term care policies

e. Specialty insurance (e.g., professional, malpractice, antiques)

f. Insurance analysis and sources of information

VI. Investments – 15%

a. Liquid assets

b. Bonds

c. Equities

d. Mutual funds and exchange traded funds

e. Other (e.g., commodities, precious metals, real estate, derivatives)

f. Sources of information

g. Time value of money

h. Asset/portfolio allocation

VII. Retirement and Estate Planning – 15%

a. Terminology (vesting, maturity, rollovers)

b. Qualified retirement accounts (e.g., IRA, Roth IRA, SEP, Keogh, 401(k), 403(b))

c. Social security benefits

d. Wills, trusts, and estate planning

e. Tax-deferred annuities

Chapter 2

Personal Finance Diagnostic Test

DIAGNOSTIC TEST ANSWER SHEET

1. Ⓐ Ⓑ Ⓒ Ⓓ

2. Ⓐ Ⓑ Ⓒ Ⓓ

3. Ⓐ Ⓑ Ⓒ Ⓓ

4. Ⓐ Ⓑ Ⓒ Ⓓ

5. Ⓐ Ⓑ Ⓒ Ⓓ

6. Ⓐ Ⓑ Ⓒ Ⓓ

7. Ⓐ Ⓑ Ⓒ Ⓓ

8. Ⓐ Ⓑ Ⓒ Ⓓ

9. Ⓐ Ⓑ Ⓒ Ⓓ

10. Ⓐ Ⓑ Ⓒ Ⓓ

11. Ⓐ Ⓑ Ⓒ Ⓓ

12. Ⓐ Ⓑ Ⓒ Ⓓ

13. Ⓐ Ⓑ Ⓒ Ⓓ

14. Ⓐ Ⓑ Ⓒ Ⓓ

15. Ⓐ Ⓑ Ⓒ Ⓓ

16. Ⓐ Ⓑ Ⓒ Ⓓ

17. Ⓐ Ⓑ Ⓒ Ⓓ

18. Ⓐ Ⓑ Ⓒ Ⓓ

19. Ⓐ Ⓑ Ⓒ Ⓓ

20. Ⓐ Ⓑ Ⓒ Ⓓ

PERSONAL FINANCE DIAGNOSTIC TEST
24 minutes—20 questions

Directions: Carefully read each of the following 20 questions. Choose the best answer to each question and fill in the corresponding circle on the answer sheet. The Answer Key and Explanations can be found following this Diagnostic Test.

---

1. Who is responsible for paying for credit counseling for debtors filing for bankruptcy?

    A. Debtors
    B. Federal government through a debt reduction program
    C. State government through a debt reduction program
    D. Debtors' creditors

2. Which of the following is subtracted from income to arrive at a person's adjusted gross income?

    A. Tax credit
    B. IRA contribution
    C. Real estate taxes
    D. Medical expenses

3. Homeowner's insurance typically does NOT cover

    A. damage from a lightning strike.
    B. equipment used to run a business from home.
    C. theft.
    D. damage from the weight of snow on a roof.

4. Mary retired after thirty years. She will receive $4,000 a month before taxes in pension benefits from her former employer for the rest of her life. What type of pension plan does her former employer have?

    A. Defined contribution plan
    B. Defined benefit plan
    C. Guaranteed plan
    D. Simplified employee pension plan

5. The asset that a borrower puts up as repayment for a loan should the borrower default is known as

A. capital.
B. credit.
C. conditions.
D. collateral.

6. Which of the following is taxable income?

A. Child support payments
B. Interest from municipal bonds
C. Tips
D. Damages received as a result of a lawsuit against a convicted drunk driver

7. Which of the following types of life insurance has no cash value?

A. Variable life
B. Universal life
C. Whole life
D. Term life

8. Using the rule of 72, approximately how long will it take to double $4,000 invested at 3 percent?

A. 8 years
B. 12 years
C. 18 years
D. 24 years

9. If a person is concerned about inflation during retirement, that person would invest in

A. deferred annuity.
B. fixed annuity.
C. variable annuity.
D. life income annuity.

10. A broker lends securities to a client who wishes to sell them now and buy them back later. This is known as a

A. margin call.
B. market order.
C. short position.
D. maintenance margin requirement.

11. Which of the following is an example of closed-end credit?

    A. Buying a pair of shoes at a shoe store

    B. A mortgage

    C. Buying a piece of furniture at a department store

    D. Paying for a doctor's services with a check

12. Which of the following provisions of health insurance policies is the most beneficial for policy holders?

    A. Internal benefits

    B. Service benefit

    C. Fixed dollar benefit

    D. Assigned benefits

13. The time value of money refers to

    A. the amount of risk versus the amount of return.

    B. buying or selling assets within a single day.

    C. buying and holding assets in anticipation of income.

    D. the increase in an amount of money as a result of interest earned.

14. Self-employed persons may lower their income tax by deducting which of the following expenses?

    A. Self-employment tax

    B. Health insurance

    C. Contribution to a Roth IRA

    D. Their state's excise tax

15. When is it better to return a leased vehicle rather than buy it when the lease is up?

    A. When the market value is less than the residual value

    B. When the car has reached its capitalized cost

    C. When the lease rate increases more than 5 percent

    D. When the end-of-lease payment is higher than the appraisal

16. Which of the following is classified as a long-term financial strategy?

    A. Saving for a down payment on a house

    B. Saving for a child's college education

    C. Buying a new car

    D. Paying off the $11,000 balance on a credit card

17. Which of the following is NOT a cost of ownership of a vehicle?

   A. Taxes on the vehicle
   B. Vehicle insurance
   C. Depreciation
   D. Buying gas

18. An example of a current liability is a(n)

   A. electric utility bill.
   B. home mortgage.
   C. car loan.
   D. eighteen-month installment loan for a new washer and dryer.

19. The cost of operation of a vehicle includes

   A. depreciation.
   B. registration.
   C. sales tax.
   D. maintenance.

20. Joint tenancy with right of survivorship is a way to

   A. avoid paying federal inheritance tax.
   B. avoid probate.
   C. ensure that property is not part of an estate for tax purposes.
   D. divide an estate equally among heirs

ANSWER KEY AND EXPLANATIONS

1. A	5. D	9. C	13. D	17. D
2. B	6. C	10. C	14. B	18. A
3. B	7. D	11. B	15. A	19. D
4. B	8. D	12. B	16. B	20. B

1. **The correct answer is A.** Under the Bankruptcy Abuse Prevention and Consumer Protection Act of 2005, those who file for bankruptcy must enroll in credit counseling before filing for bankruptcy and in a credit education course after filing for bankruptcy. The debtor pays for both. It's a federal law, but the federal government doesn't pay for the programs, so choice B is incorrect. Neither a state program (choice C) nor the debtors' creditors (choice D) are responsible for paying for credit counseling.

2. **The correct answer is B.** Adjusted gross income is income after certain deductions have been subtracted. A contribution to a filer's IRA is one of the items that is used. A tax credit (choice A) is subtracted directly from the amount of tax owed. Real estate taxes (choice C) and medical expenses (choice D) are subtracted from adjusted gross income after it has been determined.

3. **The correct answer is B.** Equipment used in a business operated out of a residence is not typically covered by a homeowner's policy. Lightning (choice A), theft (choice C), and damage from the weight of snow (choice D) are generally covered.

4. **The correct answer is B.** The scenario describes a defined benefit plan. A defined contribution plan (choice A) specifies the contribution of the employer but not the level of benefits the employee will receive at or during retirement. A guaranteed plan (choice C) is in essence what a defined benefit plan is, but that's not the correct term. A simplified employee pension plan, known as a SEP (choice D), is set up by someone who is self-employed.

5. **The correct answer is D.** Collateral is an asset that backs a borrower's promise to repay a loan. Capital (choice A) is the net worth of a borrower. Credit (choice B) is an agreement under which a person receives money, goods, or services in exchange for a promise to repay the money or pay for the good or service at a later date. Conditions (choice C) refers to economic conditions that affect a person's ability to repay a loan. Capital, collateral, and conditions, along with character and capacity, make up what is known as the "five Cs of credit."

6. **The correct answer is C.** Tips are considered taxable income. Child support (choice A), municipal bond interest (choice B), and damages from a lawsuit for personal injury or illness (choice D) are not taxed.

7. **The correct answer is D.** Term life insurance has no cash value; it pays only death benefits. Variable life and universal life insurance (choices A and B) are types of whole life policies (choice C), and all have cash values; the savings feature is a major advantage of whole life policies.

8. **The correct answer is D.** The rule of 72 is:

$$\text{Doubling Time (DT)} = \frac{72}{\text{interest rate}} \quad \text{so} \quad \frac{72}{3} = 24 \text{ years.}$$

9. **The correct answer is C.** A hedge against inflation is an advantage of variable annuities. Both variable and fixed are investment options of any type of annuity. Variable annuities are invested in equities, which, theoretically, increase their returns over time. A fixed annuity (choice B) is invested in bonds and mortgages; the rate of return is fixed, so increasing inflation will eat into the income. Deferred and life income (choices A and D) are types of annuities rather than investment options.

10. **The correct answer is C.** The question prompt describes taking a short position. A margin call (choice A) is a call from a broker to a client asking the client to increase the amount of money in his or her account for stock bought on margin; a margin call occurs when the price of the stock falls below the initial margin requirement, or percentage of the stock price invested by the client. The amount of the additional money fulfills the maintenance margin requirement (choice D). A market order (choice B) is an order to buy or sell a stock at the best available price.

11. **The correct answer is B.** Closed-end credit is a loan used for a single purchase, such as a mortgage, and must be repaid within a certain period; payments are made regularly and in equal payments. Buying store merchandise (choices A and C) or paying for a doctor's services with a check (choice D) are examples of open-end credit, which is a line of credit used for a series of purchases over time and for which the borrower is billed regularly; amounts of repayment vary depending on charges.

12. **The correct answer is B.** A service benefit states the services that the insured will receive, whereas a fixed dollar benefit (choice C) states the amount of money paid by the insurance company for each service or procedure. A service benefit is better because if a procedure costs more than the fixed dollar amount, the patient has to pay the difference. Internal benefits (choice A) is a distracter meant to seem like a possibility, but it is nonexistent. Assigned benefits (choice D) gives the insurance company the authority to pay the doctor, lab, or hospital directly.

13. **The correct answer is D.** The time value of money refers to the increase in an amount of money as a result of interest earned. The amount of risk an investor is willing to take versus the amount of return (choice A) refers to opportunity costs. Buying or selling assets within a single day (choice B) is the practice of day trading. Investing in equities involves buying and holding assets in anticipation of income (choice C).

14. **The correct answer is B.** A self-employed person can take a deduction for health insurance. Choice A is Social Security. Every worker must pay this tax, and it is not deductible; a self-employed person pays at a rate of 13.3 percent in Social Security and Medicare taxes. A Roth IRA (choice C) is tax-deferred and has no impact on income tax. An excise tax (choice D) is paid on certain goods, such as gas, tires, and communication services; it is a state and federal tax and is not deductible (but a sales tax is deductible).

15. **The correct answer is A.** There is no profit to be made on a car that you'll pay more to the dealer to buy than you'll be able to sell in the marketplace, so choice A is the best answer. Choice B is incorrect because the capitalized cost is the price that the dealer puts on the car to lease it; it is typically 96 percent of the list price. Choice C is also incorrect because according to the question, the lease is over; also, the lease rate is set when the lease is signed, so it doesn't go up or down over the life of the lease. The end-of-lease payment (choice D) has to be paid regardless of whether the lessee buys the car at the end of the lease; this is a provision of an open-end lease, not a closed-end lease.

16. **The correct answer is B.** Saving for a child's college education is considered a long-term financial strategy. Saving for a down payment (choice A) and possibly paying off a large credit card debt (choice D) are medium-term strategies. A medium-term strategy typically takes more than a year but fewer than five. Buying a new car (choice C) is a short-term strategy.

17. **The correct answer is D.** Buying gas is a cost of operation. Taxes on the vehicle (choice A), vehicle insurance (choice B), and depreciation (choice C) are costs of ownership of a vehicle.

18. **The correct answer is A.** A current liability is one that must be paid off within a year. An electric bill is an example of a current liability. Choices B, C, and D are noncurrent liabilities, though the installment payments due this year for the mortgage, car loan, and new appliances are current liabilities.

19. **The correct answer is D.** Maintenance is part of the cost of operation of a vehicle. Depreciation (choice A), registration (choice B), and sales tax (choice C) are part of the cost of ownership.

20. **The correct answer is B.** Property owned as a joint tenancy with right of survivorship passes to the surviving owner or owners without having to pass through probate court. Choice A is incorrect because there is no federal inheritance tax, though some states do levy an inheritance tax. Choice C describes an irrevocable trust, and choice D describes the per capita division of an estate.

DIAGNOSTIC TEST ASSESSMENT GRID

Now that you've completed the diagnostic test and read through the answer explanations, you can use your results to target your studying. Find the question numbers from the diagnostic test that you answered incorrectly and highlight or circle them below. Then focus extra attention on the sections dealing with those topics.

Personal Finance		
Content Area	**Topic**	**Question #**
Foundations of Financial Planning	• Economic terminology • Financial goals and values • Budgeting and financial statements • Cash management • Institutional aspects of financial planning	16, 18
Credit and Debt	• Credit and debit cards • Installment loans • Interest calculations • Federal credit laws • Creditworthiness, credit scoring, and reporting • Bankruptcy	1, 5, 11
Major Purchases	• Auto, furniture, appliances • Housing	15, 17, 19

Content Area	Topic	Question #
Taxes	• Payroll • Income • IRS and audits • Estate and gift • Tax planning/estimating • Progressive vs. regressive • Other (excise, property, sales, gas) • Tax professionals	2, 6, 14
Insurance	• Risk management • Life policies • Property and liability policies • Health, disability, and long-term care policies • Specialty insurance (e.g., professional, mal- practice, antiques) • Insurance analysis and sources of information	3, 7, 12
Investments	• Liquid assets • Bonds • Equities • Mutual funds and exchange traded funds • Other (e.g., commodities, precious metals, real estate, derivatives) • Sources of information • Time value of money • Asset/portfolio allocation	8, 10, 13
Retirement and Estate Planning	• Terminology (vesting, maturity, rollovers) • Qualified retirement accounts (e.g., IRA, Roth IRA, SEP, Keogh, 401(k), 403(b)) • Social security benefits • Wills, trusts, and estate planning • Tax-deferred annuities	4, 9, 20

Chapter 3

Personal Finance Subject Review

OVERVIEW

- **Foundations of Financial Planning**
- **Credit and Debt**
- **Major Purchases**
- **Taxes**
- **Insurance**
- **Investments**
- **Retirement and Estate Planning**
- **Summing It Up**

FOUNDATIONS OF FINANCIAL PLANNING

A person's life typically intertwines nonfinancial and financial goals. In order to achieve nonfinancial goals, such as having a satisfying career, a happy marriage, and a family, a person typically needs a certain amount of money. The amount depends on what satisfies a person. One person may be satisfied only with a twenty-room mansion, while another may be perfectly happy in a studio apartment. Financial planning is managing one's money in order to achieve economic satisfaction.

Economic Terminology

Personal finance refers to how you manage your money, including your income, expenses, and savings. When you focus on managing your personal finances, you have a better grasp on where your money is going and what changes you can make to meet your future financial goals. Here are some common terms related to personal finance:

- **Economics:** The study of the production, distribution, and consumption of goods and services
- **Long-term Goal:** A goal that will take at least several years to achieve
- **Financial Planning:** Setting short-, medium-, and long-range goals and then collecting and analyzing income and expenditure information to determine how to meet these goals
- **Financial Risk:** The chance that an individual, business, or government will not be able to return the money invested with them
- **Retirement Accounts:** Accounts that allow individuals to save money toward retirement on a tax-deferred basis
- **Risk:** The chance of losing invested money

Financial Goals and Values

Financial goals involve **consumption** and **savings**; consumption may be current or future—i.e., what you need/want now versus what you will need/want at some later time. The ability to obtain those needs/wants depends on earnings, savings, and investments. Therefore, financial goals can be categorized based on **short-term**, **medium-term**, and **long-term** timeframes.

- **Short-term goals** should take no longer than about one year to reach. For example, you may plan to pay off the $2,500 balance on your credit card.
- **Medium-term goals** should be attainable within one to five years. An example of this type of goal would be planning to save $20,000 in the next five years for a down payment on a house.
- **Long-term goals** will take more than five years to reach. Saving for retirement or for a child's education are examples of long-term goals.

Goals may also be categorized by type as follows:

- **Consumable-product goals:** purchasing food, clothing, entertainment
- **Durable-product goals:** buying "big-ticket" items such as a home, cars, and appliances
- **Intangible-product goals:** paying for education (such as earning a degree), leisure, digitized content

Financial goals change in importance as a person moves through each stage of the life cycle. Areas that require people to set financial goals include debt, insurance, investing, retirement, estate, and career.

Facets of Financial Planning

Financial Goals	Evaluate and plan major outlays
	Manage credit
	Secure adequate insurance coverage
	Establish savings/investment programs
	Manage employee benefits
	Reduce taxes
	Implement retirement program
	Minimize estate taxes
Budget	Monitor and control income, living expenses, purchases, and savings on a monthly basis
Financial Statements	Actual financial results: • Balance sheet • Income and expense statement

Budgeting and Financial Statements

Once the goals are set, a person needs a plan to achieve them, that is, a budget that allocates money to different items, such as rent or mortgage payments, food, utilities, and savings. The budgeting process is typically done on a monthly basis and includes the following steps: estimating income; allocating for fixed expenses; allocating for variable expenses, such as car repairs; allocating for savings, and allocating for an emergency fund. The next two steps are ongoing: entering the actual amounts next to the estimated amounts in order to see variances between budgeted and actual, and then analyzing the monthly results to determine how accurate the original budget was and what needs to be changed in order to stay on track to achieve the financial goals.

The Budgeting Process

Assess Your Current Situation	In this preliminary phase, your main tasks are to: • Measure your current financial position • Determine your personal needs, values, and life situation
Plan Your Financial Direction	The actual budgeting activities occur in this phase: **Step 1:** Set financial goals **Step 2:** Estimate income **Step 3:** Budget an emergency fund and savings **Step 4:** Budget fixed expenses **Step 5:** Budget variable expense
Implement Your Budget	As you select and use your budgeting system **Step 6:** Record spending amounts
Execute Your Budget Program	In the final phase of the process, you need to: **Step 7:** Review spending and saving patterns With the completion of the process, possible revisions of financial goals and budget allocations should be considered.

Corporations have financial statements, and individuals, couples, and families can have financial statements as well. The first item should be a **balance sheet**, which lists assets minus liabilities (debt) to show net worth. Assets include **liquid assets**—cash and anything that can be quickly turned into cash—real estate, personal property, and investments. Liabilities are both short-term (less than one year) and long-term, also called **noncurrent liabilities**.

The second type of statement is a **cash flow statement**; it shows inflows and outflows of money, or what came in and what went out. Inflows include salaries, interest, and dividends. A cash flow statement is a useful tool for planning a household budget.

Cash Management

Should savings be kept in a savings account or a certificate of deposit? Should money be deposited in a commercial bank, online, or at a credit union? These are questions that are part of creating a **cash management system**, a way to have cash, or the equivalent, handy for regular purchases and for emergencies.

The typical places to hold cash are regular checking accounts, interest-bearing checking accounts, savings accounts, money market deposit/demand accounts, money market mutual funds, CDs, and Series EE and Series I US government savings bonds. The first four have no restrictions on withdrawals. Mutual funds typically have restrictions on the number of checks that may be written each month, and CDs carry a penalty for early withdrawal. Series I US government savings bonds are interest-bearing bonds intended to be long-term investments. They can be cashed in after one year but doing so before five years will forfeit the last three months of interest accrued.

Banks and other financial institutions offer services to meet a variety of needs. These fall into four primary categories:

1. *Savings:* Savings involves safe storage of funds for future use.
2. *Cash availability and payment services:* Payment services give the ability to transfer money to others for conducting business. Checking accounts and other payment methods are commonly called **demand deposits**.
3. *Borrowing:* Borrowing refers to credit alternatives available for short- and long-term needs.
4. *Investments and other financial services:* These include insurance protection, investments, real estate purchases, tax assistance, and financial planning.

Institutional Aspects of Financial Planning

Deciding on the institutions, that is, financial services organizations and professionals, that a person will need is also part of financial planning. The choices of depository institutions include commercial banks, both bricks-and-mortar and online; savings and loan associations; mutual savings banks; and credit unions. Other companies that provide financial services include life insurance companies, mutual funds, finance companies, mortgage companies, brokerage houses, and financial planners and investment advisors.

Financial planners are licensed and regulated by the Certified Financial Planner Board of Standards, Inc. Not all individuals who call themselves financial planners are licensed, so a person looking for a financial planner should be aware of this. An **investment adviser** is a legal term, and investment advisers are regulated by either the Securities and Exchange Commission (SEC) or a state securities regulator, depending on the amount of assets the person manages. Stock and bond brokers are regulated by the SEC. They must register with the SEC and also be members of the Financial Industry Regulatory Authority (FINRA).

There are a number of laws that regulate the securities industry. Federal laws such as the Dodd-Frank Act of 2010 resulted from abuses by financial institutions during the first decade of the twenty-first century, which caused the Great Recession.

Financial Institutions Services	
Cash Availability	**Payment Services**
Check cashing	Checking account
ATM/debit cards	Online payments
Traveler's checks	Cashier's checks
Foreign currency exchange	Money orders
Savings Services	**Credit Services**
Regular savings account	Credit cards, cash advances
Money market account	Auto loans, education loans
Certificates of deposit	Mortgages
US savings bond	Home equity loans
Investment Services	**Other Services**
Individual retirement accounts (IRA)	Insurance, trust services
Brokerage service	Tax preparations
Investment advice	Safe deposit boxes
Mutual funds	Budget counseling

CREDIT AND DEBT

The world—at least the United States—seems to run on credit today. Mailing a package at the post office? Use a credit card. Buying tickets to the movies? Use a debit card. Buying furniture at a department store? Use the store's charge card and be eligible for one-year deferred payment. From paying for a fast-food meal to buying a new car, a person never needs to have cash on hand, just a credit or debit card. With all the ease of using credit, it may take something as disastrous as bankruptcy to bring home the fact that credit comes with a price.

Credit and Debit Cards

Types of Credit

Consumer credit is use of credit by individuals, that is, an individual's promise to pay later for the use of a good or service now. The reasons for using credit are many: convenience, the ability to consume more than could be afforded based solely on income, as a hedge against inflation, and for emergencies. The disadvantages of using credit are also many: the temptation to spend more than a person has, the consequences of overspending, the cost of credit, and limitation on future spending power because of the cost of credit for past purchases.

Closed-end credit is credit used for a specific purchase for a specific period and for a specific amount of money, such as purchasing a vehicle on a three-year loan. Closed-end credit may be in the form of installment sales credit, installment cash credit, and single lump-sum credit. Repayment for the first two is in regular amounts over a period of time.

Open-end credit is a line of credit that enables a consumer to make a series of purchases over a period of time as long as the consumer doesn't go over the amount of the line of credit. The consumer must repay the amount in regular payments, but the payments may be of varying amounts as long as the payments meet the minimum amount stated by the card issuer. This is also known as a **revolving credit** account. Some stores, such as a cleaner, for example, may offer customers regular charge accounts: the customer charges purchases during the month and then is sent a bill at the end of the month that is due in full.

Open-end credit instruments include credit/smart cards, a debit card, and a home equity line of credit. A travel and entertainment card must be paid in full each month, unlike credit cards, which can be paid in installments.

It's important to research any extra perks or protections a credit card may offer. Some of the most attractive bonuses can help the cardholder save money or protect them from certain losses. Among the most valuable perks include those that offer protection if the card is used to purchase something that breaks or fails to perform as promised or for which the merchant doesn't provide the promised goods or services.

Another important consideration when researching a credit card is the grace period. A **grace period** is the amount of time (if any) after a purchase in which you can pay off the balance without incurring an interest charge. If a credit card does offer a grace period, it must be at least 21 days, as required by the Credit CARD Act of 2009 (a federal law governing many rules related to credit cards and often referred to as the credit cardholder's bill of rights).

There are some important distinctions between credit cards and debit cards. Among the most significant differences: with a debit card purchase, the transaction amount is immediately deducted from your account and there is no grace period or "float" (if there aren't sufficient funds in the account, the transaction may be declined or may result in overdraft charges). Also, losses from a stolen credit card are capped at $50, whereas losses with a stolen debit card are only capped at that amount if the card holder notifies the bank within two days. The cap can rise to $500 for losses incurred if the bank is notified within two and sixty days.

Installment Loans

An installment loan is a loan in which there are a set number of scheduled payments over time. Many different types of loans are installment loans. These include the following:

- **Student Loans:** Student loans are a type of installment loan. With student loans, you receive a set amount of money for your educational costs, and then, once out of school, you pay back the loans by paying a set amount each month. Student loans also allow you the option of deferring your payments when you are unemployed for a period of time, but you will have to resume your payments once you are employed again.
- **Mortgage Loans:** When you take out a mortgage loan, you are able to finance the purchase of your home and pay back the loan over a set number of years. It is important that you stay current with your payments or you risk losing your home and damaging your credit.
- **Car Loans:** When you need a car but do not have enough money to pay up front, taking out a car loan can be ideal. However, similar to mortgage loans, if you do not pay back the money as scheduled, your car can be repossessed and your credit would be damaged.

Interest Calculations

Interest is what you pay to borrow money using a loan, credit card, or line of credit. It is calculated at either a fixed or variable rate that is expressed as a percentage of the amount you borrow, tied to a specific time period. This can be classified as simple interest or compound interest. **Simple interest** is calculated only on the principal amount of a loan. **Compound interest** is calculated on the principal amount and also on the accumulated interest of previous periods and thus is regarded as "interest on interest." This compounding effect can make a big difference in the amount of interest payable on a loan as interest is calculated on a compound rather than simple basis.

Simple Interest

The formula for calculating simple interest is:

Simple Interest = Principal × Interest Rate × Term of the Loan

$$I = P \times i \times n$$

If simple interest is charged at 3 percent on a $15,000 loan that is taken out for a three-year period, the total amount of interest payable by the borrower is calculated as:

Simple Interest = $15,000 \times 0.03 \times 3 = \$1,350$.

Interest on this loan is payable at $450 annually or $1,350 over the three-year loan term.

Compound Interest

The formula for calculating compound interest is:

Compound Interest = Total amount of Principal and Interest in future (or Future Value) less Principal amount at present (or Present Value)

$$= [P(1 + i)n] - P$$
$$= P[(1 + i)n - 1]$$

where P = Principal, i = annual interest rate in percentage terms, and n = number of compounding periods.

Continuing with the values of the simple interest example, what would be the amount of interest if it is charged on a compound basis? In this case it would be:

$15,000 [(1 + 0.03) 3] - 1 = \$15,000 [1.092727 - 1] = \$1,390.91$.

While the total interest payable over the three-year period of this loan is $1,390.91, unlike simple interest, the interest amount is not the same for all three years because compound interest also takes into consideration accumulated interest of previous periods. Interest payable at the end of each year is shown in the following table:

Year	Opening Balance (*P*)	Interest @ 3%	Closing Balance (*P* + *i*)
1	$15,000.00	$450.00	$15,450.00
2	$15,450.00	$463.50	$15,913.50
3	$15,913.50	$477.41	$16,390.91
	Total Interest	**$1,390.91**	

Compounding Periods

When calculating compound interest, the number of compounding periods makes a significant difference. The basic rule is that the higher the number of compounding periods, the greater the amount of compound interest. So for every $100 of a loan over a certain period, the amount of interest accrued at 10 percent annually will be lower than interest accrued at 5 percent semiannually, which will, in turn, be lower than interest accrued at 2.5 percent quarterly.

In the formula for calculating compound interest, the variables i and n have to be adjusted if the number of compounding periods is more than one a year. That is, i has to be divided by the number of compounding periods per year, and n has to be multiplied by the number of compounding periods. Therefore, for a 10-year loan at 10 percent where interest is compounded semiannually (number of compounding periods = 2), $i = 5\%$ (i.e., 10% / 2) and $n = 20$ (i.e., 10 × 2).

The following table demonstrates the difference that the number of compounding periods can make over time for a $10,000 loan taken for a 10-year period.

Compounding Frequency	Number of Compounding Periods	Values of *i* and *n*	Total Interest
Annually	1	$i = 10\%, n = 10$	$15,937.42
Semiannually	2	$i = 5\%, n = 20$	$16,532.98
Quarterly	4	$i = 2.5\%, n = 40$	$16,850.64
Monthly	12	$i = 0.833\%, n = 120$	$17,070.41

Federal Credit Laws

Enacted in 1971, the Fair Credit Reporting Act (FCRA) was the first federal law to regulate how personal information is used by a private business. This act safeguards your credit by requiring consumer reporting agencies to follow certain standards. It gives you the right to a free credit report annually, protected access, and accurate reporting. This act also gives you the right to have inaccuracies fixed in a timely manner, as well as the right to sue and seek damages for violations.

The Fair Credit Reporting Act contains three smaller acts: The Credit CARD Act, the Dodd-Frank Act, and the Fair and Accurate Credit Transactions Act. These deal with the accountability of credit card companies and your rights if someone steals your identity.

The Credit CARD Act

The Credit CARD Act is often called the Credit Cardholders Bill of Rights. President Barack Obama signed the bill into law in May 2009. Many of the most significant provisions of the law took effect in February 2010. The law has two main purposes:

1. *Fairness*: Prohibits certain practices that are unfair or abusive, such as hiking up the rate on an existing balance or allowing a consumer to go over limit and then imposing an over-limit fee.
2. *Transparency*: Rates and fees are required to be transparent so consumers can understand how much they are paying for their credit card and can compare the costs of different cards.

The Dodd-Frank Act

Dodd-Frank is a law that places major regulations on the financial industry. It grew out of the Great Recession with the intention of preventing another collapse of a major financial institution like Lehman Brothers. Dodd-Frank is also geared toward protecting consumers with rules such as keeping borrowers from abusive lending and mortgage practices by banks. It became a law in 2010 and was named after Senator Christopher J. Dodd (D-CT) and US Representative Barney Frank (D-MA), who were the sponsors of the legislation.

The Fair and Accurate Credit Transactions Act

The Fair and Accurate Credit Transaction Act of 2003 (FACTA) added sections to the federal Fair Credit Reporting Act intended primarily to help consumers fight identity theft. Accuracy, privacy, limits on information sharing, and new consumer rights to disclosure are included in FACTA.

Creditworthiness, Credit Scoring, and Reporting

Credit comes in many different shapes and sizes, including mortgages, loans, overdrafts, and credit cards. In most cases you will have to pay an agreed amount back every month with interest. Your **credit report** is a history of your credit accounts and payment activity. It also includes your basic personal information and certain types of public data, such as whether you have declared bankruptcy or are involved in a lawsuit. Your **credit score** is a rating that quantifies the potential risk you pose to a lender or merchant.

A **FICO score** is a credit score developed by the Fair Isaac Corporation (FICO), a company that specializes in what is known as "predictive analytics," which means they take information and analyze it to predict what is likely to happen. The FICO score range is 300–850, with the higher number representing less risk to the lender or insurer. To create credit scores, FICO uses information provided by one of the three major credit-reporting agencies:

1. Equifax
2. Experian
3. TransUnion

You are legally entitled to obtain a copy of your credit report from each of the three nationwide credit agencies once a year by visiting **www.annualcreditreport.com**, a site authorized by the federal government to provide the information free of charge.

Consumers with high FICO scores (usually around 760 or higher, though every lender is different) are likely to get the best rates when they borrow, as well as the best discounts on insurance. When qualifying a person for credit, a creditor looks for the five Cs of creditworthiness:

1. Character
2. Capacity
3. Capital
4. Collateral
5. Conditions

Character

When lenders evaluate character, they look at stability: how long you have lived at your current address, how long you have been in your current job, and whether you have a good record of paying your bills on time and in full. If you want a loan for your business, the lender may consider your experience and track record in your business and industry to evaluate how trustworthy you are to repay a loan.

Capacity

Capacity refers to considering your other debts and expenses when determining your ability to repay the loan. Creditors evaluate your debt-to-income ratio, that is, how much you owe compared to how much you earn. The lower your ratio, the more confident creditors will be in your capacity to repay the money you borrow. Your monthly obligations related to payoff debt—such as payments for mortgages, auto loans, student loans, or other debt—are all taken into consideration when calculating your debt-to-income ratio.

Capital

Capital refers to your net worth—the value of your assets minus your liabilities. In simple terms, how much you own (for example, car, real estate, cash, and investments) minus how much you owe.

Collateral

Collateral refers to any asset of a borrower, for example, a home, that a lender has a right to take ownership of and use to pay the debt if the borrower is unable to make the loan payments as agreed. Some lenders may require a guarantee in addition to collateral; a guarantee means that another person signs a document promising to repay the loan if you cannot.

Conditions

Lenders consider a number of outside circumstances that may affect the borrower's financial situation and ability to repay, such as what is happening in the local economy. If the borrower is a business, the lender may evaluate the financial health of the borrower's industry, their local market, and their competition.

This last C is outside the control of the consumer applying for credit; "conditions" refers to the stability of the person's job and employer. A creditor checks an applicant's FICO score, which considers length of credit history, on-time payment history, current amounts owed, types of credit in the credit history, and inquiries from new credit sources. If a person has a low score, there are ways to improve creditworthiness: pay bills on time, increase capital, don't move debt from one creditor to another, don't open new credit accounts, and reduce credit card balances. It's also important for consumers to check their credit scores several times per year to correct any mistakes.

Bankruptcy

The Bankruptcy Code was established in 1978 and underwent a major overhaul in 2005. At that time, the Bankruptcy Abuse Prevention and Consumer Protection Act of 2005 was hailed as an important measure to ensure that people do not use bankruptcy court as a revolving door that allows them to spend without a thought to the future, go into overwhelming debt, file for bankruptcy to escape paying off their debts, and then do it all over again.

There are two forms of personal bankruptcy: straight bankruptcy and the wage-earner plan. Straight bankruptcy is filed under **Chapter 7** of the Bankruptcy Code, and wage-earner bankruptcy is filed under **Chapter 13**.

Chapter 7—Straight Bankruptcy

As part of Chapter 7 bankruptcy, a debtor must enumerate for the court his or her assets as well as list creditors with the amounts owed and the debtor's income, property, and monthly expenses. In Chapter 7, the debtor must sell most of his or her assets. Exceptions allow the debtor to keep part of his or her equity in a home or personal property such as a car or truck. In addition, Social Security payments and unemployment compensation may be exempted, as well as equipment used in skilled work.

Most debts are wiped clean, but the price is more than losing many or most of one's assets. Credit reports carry notice of Chapter 7 bankruptcies for ten years. A Chapter 7 bankruptcy can be used only once every eight years.

Chapter 13—Wage-Earner Plan

As part of Chapter 13 bankruptcy, the debtor does not have to sell his or her assets to pay debts. Instead, the debtor works out a plan with court approval to pay off current debts with future earnings over a five-year period. This form of bankruptcy is used only for debtors with a regular income. Credit reports carry Chapter 13 bankruptcies for seven years.

Additional Provisions of the 2005 Act

There are a number of additional provisions in the 2005 Act. Among which, debtors must undergo credit counseling before filing for bankruptcy. Debtors must also take a financial education course after entering bankruptcy. The debtor is required to pay for both. Other costs involved in filing for bankruptcy include court costs, trustees' fees and costs, and attorneys' fees.

In general, certain debts and payments survive a bankruptcy:

- Income taxes
- Alimony payments
- Child support payments
- Student loans
- Any debts deliberately contracted with the idea of filing for bankruptcy
- Court awards, such as restitution of embezzled funds or damages awarded as a result of driving while under the influence of alcohol. Court awards may be discharged in a Chapter 13 filing, but not in Chapter 7.

As noted above, the consequences of filing for bankruptcy are far more than losing one's material assets. Bankruptcy records follow the filer around for seven or ten years. This can affect a person's ability to qualify for credit or a job and to buy insurance.

MAJOR PURCHASES

The largest purchase that consumers typically make is a home. The next largest is a vehicle, but consumer durable goods also have hefty price tags. Comparison shopping involves a trade-off in time versus money, but it is a smart strategy when thousands of dollars are involved. Buying decisions—whether for cars or stocks—involve the same basic steps: gathering information, evaluating alternatives, determining what a person is willing to pay, and financing/paying for the purchase.

Purchasing an Automobile

As part of gathering information for the purchase of a vehicle, the buyer needs to identify the reasons that he or she wants or needs a car. Next, the buyer should consider whether to buy or lease a car and, if buying, whether to buy a new or used car. In signing a lease, the lessee agrees to pay a small upfront fee—the security deposit—and monthly payments for use of the vehicle over a period of time. Vehicle leases usually run for three, four, or five years, and at the end of the lease, the lessee may buy the car. Otherwise, the car must be returned to the lessor.

Evaluating Leasing Versus Buying

Leasing a car rather than buying a car on credit reduces the initial outlay and also incurs smaller periodic payments. An additional benefit to leasing a car is intangible. The lessee may be able to lease a car that is more expensive than what the lessee could afford to buy. However, this can be a negative because a more expensive car depreciates more, and finance charges may be higher. A lessee also has no equity in the vehicle. However, the lessee is required to pay for maintenance, mileage over the amount stated in the leasing agreement, some types of repairs, and a penalty for breaking the lease, that is, turning the car in early.

To determine whether to buy or lease, a comparison can be made based on three basic pieces of information: initial costs, monthly payments, and final expenses to pay off the lease. Even considering the time value of money, that is, the interest earned on the difference between the smaller amount of the periodic payments on the lease and the larger amount of payments on the car loan, the buyer typically comes out better.

Determining Purchase Price

If a buyer decides to buy rather than lease, the question becomes whether to get a new or a used vehicle. Some buyers purchase only used cars because of the depreciation factor. The greatest depreciation occurs in the first two or three years of ownership, so these buyers prefer to purchase cars that are two or three years old. The price of a used car is determined by mileage, condition, features and options, and demand in the marketplace for the make and model. To determine the price that a buyer is willing to pay, he or she may check the prices in car ads and online dealers as well as *Edmund's Used Cars* and *Kelley Blue Book*. On the lot, a buyer should also check the "Buyers Guide" sticker on the car.

One item to look for is whether the car is sold "as is" or is still under warranty. If there is no warranty stated but the car isn't explicitly being sold "as is," there may still be some protections provided under implied warranties. Buyers should be leery of purchasing a used car "as is," because they can be taking a risk that they will incur repair expenses for existing issues. Some states prohibit dealers from selling cars "as is," and a few states also have lemon laws (federal lemon laws generally only apply to new car sales) so buyers should research applicable laws in their area.

Any used car should be checked by the buyer's mechanic to ensure that it is in good working condition.

If the decision is to buy a new car, a buyer should become familiar with the following information:

- **Monroney Sticker Price:** Price that includes the base price, manufacturer's installed options with manufacturer's suggested retail price, transportation charge from the manufacturer to the dealer, fuel economy
- **Base Price:** Price without the options
- **Invoice Price:** Cost to the dealer, which is less than the sticker price

TIP: The difference between the sticker price and the invoice price is the amount available for negotiation.

Financing

In analyzing financing options, a buyer should consider down payment, annual percentage rate (APR), finance charge, and length of the loan. The larger the down payment, the less the risk of paying off a loan on a car that is worth less than what is owed.

Cost of Ownership and Cost of Operation

The **cost of ownership** includes taxes on the vehicle, vehicle insurance, vehicle registration with the state, depreciation, and the finance charges associated with buying on credit, if the vehicle is not bought with cash.

The **cost of operation** includes buying gas, doing regular maintenance, and replacing brakes, tires, and other major parts as needed. There may also be other charges, such as renting a garage or space in a parking lot.

Car Warranties

Manufacturers provide warranties on new cars. The warranties are limited by miles driven, number of years, and the parts covered. A typical warranty is three years or 36,000 miles. In terms of parts covered, the drive train, engine, and transmission, as well as basic parts, are covered. Used cars may or may not have warranties, but this information must be stated in the "Buyers Guide."

Housing

Like buying or leasing a vehicle, housing has its own question: rent or buy? Each has its advantages and disadvantages, and each requires identifying needs and wants as well as opportunity costs and trade-offs. Factors that come into play in the decision are assumptions about whether housing prices will increase or decrease; whether returns on financial investments will remain steady, fall, or rise in the future; and what potential tax advantages will be. Because of the costs involved in buying and selling housing, the time that the buyer expects to remain in the home is also a factor.

Renting: Advantages and Disadvantages

The advantages of renting a home are mobility, little or no personal or financial responsibility for maintenance or repairs, and the lower initial cost of paying only a security deposit. The disadvantages are inability to derive financial benefits from ownership (tax deductions, increasing equity stake), the likelihood of rent increases over time, and lease restrictions on use of the rental property.

Home Ownership: Advantages and Disadvantages

Advantages of buying a home include tax deductions for mortgage interest and property taxes, capital gain that is probably not taxable because of tax adjustments, and fewer restrictions on how the property can be used. Disadvantages are limited mobility, costs associated with maintenance and repairs, high initial costs, and loss of potential interest earned on the money used for the down payment and closing costs. Buying makes better economic sense in the long term, though renting in the short term means lower initial costs.

In choosing the type of housing to buy, a buyer should consider two sets of factors. One set is the property's size, condition, location, and potential for an increase in value over time. Balanced against these factors are the price, current mortgage rates, amount possible for a down payment, and cost of mortgage payments, insurance, and property taxes on a monthly basis.

The Buying Process

Purchasing a home includes a number of steps, some of which are undertaken simultaneously: determining an amount to spend, determining the down payment, identifying a location in which to begin the housing search, choosing a real estate agent, identifying a property, making an offer and negotiating the price, signing the contract, employing a home inspector, choosing a lender, providing the fee and documentation for a mortgage application, title search by the buyer's attorney, property appraisal by the lender, mortgage approval, choosing title insurance, and the closing.

One issue for buyers in determining the mortgage amount is whether to prepay **points**, which are a lender's discount on the mortgage. Each point is equal to one percent of the amount of the loan. The more points that are prepaid, the lower the mortgage amount and payments. Prepaying points makes more sense the longer the buyer intends to own a property.

Types of Mortgages

Longer-term mortgages have smaller monthly payments. Also, larger down payments result in smaller monthly payments. An overriding factor may be the interest rate. Rates on long-term mortgages such as the 30-year fixed will be higher than a 5/1 adjustable rate mortgage (a fixed rate for 5 years that then adjusts every year). The lender assumes the risk that rates will rise over 30 years and the lender will be out the increase in the value of the money that he or she would otherwise receive from lending at the higher rates.

Depending on the amount of money that the buyer has to put down, the mortgage lender may require that the buyer take out mortgage insurance. **Mortgage insurance** is a guarantee that the lender will not lose money if the buyer defaults on the loan. **Private mortgage insurance (PMI)** is required if a buyer has less than 20 percent to put down on a home. Once the equity reaches 20 percent, the PMI is discontinued.

Most mortgages are referred to as **conventional mortgages**, and the terms typically run 30, 20, or 15 years. The mortgaged property serves as collateral. Fannie Mae and Freddie Mac are government-sponsored entities (GSE) that buy mortgages from mortgage lenders in order to return money to the mortgage market and encourage homeownership. A **conforming conventional mortgage** is one that is guaranteed by Freddie Mac or Fannie Mae. A **nonconforming mortgage** is one that cannot be sold to Freddie or Fannie because it doesn't meet the organization's requirements, for example, it is over the loan threshold.

The major formats for mortgages are **fixed rate** and **adjustable**, or **variable rate**, but there are a variety of other types of mortgages as can be seen in the following chart:

Mortgage Types

Mortgage	Advantage	Disadvantage
Fixed Rate: 30-, 20-, 15-year Term; Conventional	• Same monthly payment over the life of the mortgage • Amount of the payment that goes to the principal increases and the amount paid toward interest decreases over time (known as **amortization**) • Ability to prepay the balance in order to refinance	• Locked into a rate when mortgage rates are falling • Cost of refinancing to take advantage of falling rates • May have prepayment penalty
Adjustable Rate (ARM): 3/1, 5/1, 7/1; Two-Step; Hybrid	• Fluctuation of monthly payments annually after a set number of years at a fixed rate, though some types of ARMs may reset monthly or semiannually (known as the **interest rate adjustment period**) • Initially lower rate than fixed mortgages • Protection against huge increases in interest rate from one adjustment period to another (known as a **rate cap**) • Limit on increases in monthly payments	• Need to re-budget with each rate adjustment • Payment cap: may result in lower monthly payments than needed to repay the loan by the end of the loan term; may require large payment at end of loan term, longer term, or higher monthly payments later (known as **negative amortization**) • Cost of refinancing if mortgagor chooses to prepay and refinance

Mortgage	Advantage	Disadvantage
Balloon ARM: 3-, 5-, 7-Year Term	• Fluctuation of monthly payments after each interest rate adjustment • Payment of interest only so the payments are lower	• Entire principal owed at the end of the loan term
Interest-Only	• Initial period when interest only is paid on the loan	• Repayment period begins and mortgage is amortized over the new shorter period; increase in monthly payments
Convertible ARM	• Allows conversion of ARM to fixed rate after a certain time • Rate set in original ARM mortgage	• Requires fee • Refinancing may be better deal depending on interest rate and fee
Balloon Loan: 5-, 7-year Term	• Fixed monthly payments over the life of the loan	• Large payment required at the end of the term of the loan
Graduated Payment Mortgage; Graduated Equity Mortgage (GEM)	• Fixed rate • GEM: increases applied to principal only • Useful for young homebuyers who expect to see their incomes increase	• Amount of payments increases over time
Shared Equity; Shared Appreciation	• Large personal down payment unnecessary • Part of the down payment is borrowed in return for giving a share in the property to the lender	• At end of term, lender gets a share of the profit on the property in proportion to the amount lent—regardless of whether the borrower sells the house

In reviewing ARMs, it's important to check the rate cap and the payment cap. The **annual rate cap** limits the amount that an interest rate may increase, and it may also put a floor on how far a rate may decrease. Typically, an annual cap is no more than 2 percentage points per adjustment period. An **aggregate rate cap**, or **life-of-loan cap**, is the limit that a rate may rise during the life of the mortgage. Typically, this is no more than 6 percentage points overall. A **payment cap** limits how much the monthly payment can be increased.

Additional Financing Options

There are a variety of financing possibilities in addition to mortgages, such as the buy-down, which is a form of financing that builders of a newly constructed house offer to buyers. The builder pays a percentage of monthly mortgage payments for the first year or two.

When a buyer is also a seller and hasn't closed on the sale of his or her current home but must close on the new home, the person will use a **bridge loan**, also called a **swing loan** or **temporary loan**. Many homeowners use the equity in their homes to pay for other large-ticket items such as a new car or a kitchen renovation. These lines of credit are in essence a second mortgage on their homes and add a monthly payment to their budgets.

Reverse mortgages take money out of the equity in a home. They are available only to homeowners over 62 years of age. The money is repaid at the time of the sale of the home.

Over the course of a 30-year mortgage, interest rates may fluctuate wildly depending on the state of the economy. Refinancing may be a good option if a new mortgage can reduce the interest rate by at least one percentage point. In calculating whether to refinance, a homeowner should consider the cost of refinancing, which may be $2,500, versus the amount of savings in monthly payments to determine how long it will take to make up the refinancing costs.

Selling a Home

Up to this point, we've been talking about buying housing, but selling housing also requires information gathering and a series of decisions. The first decision, of course, is to sell and the next is at what price. The local government assessment for tax purposes is one indicator and another is the recent sale prices of comparable homes, known as comps, in your immediate area.

Sellers typically use real estate agents, though about 13 percent choose to save the real estate commission and sell their homes themselves. An advantage of using an agent who belongs to the Multiple Listing Service (MLS) is that the property can be shown by a number of different agencies. Using an agent also means that a property will be showcased on the agency's website.

There are a variety of agencies for selling real estate. A **buyer agency** represents buyers only. A **dual agency** may represent both buyers and sellers. To avoid conflicts of interest in a dual agency, an agent may use a designated agent in the same office to represent either the buyer or seller in the transaction. A **transaction brokerage** or **facilitative brokerage** does not represent the interests of either a seller or a buyer but simply shows properties to a buyer and assists in the general real estate process.

Other Major Purchases

Other than housing, a vehicle is probably the most expensive single item a consumer will buy. Vehicles are part of a category known as **consumer durables** that includes such large-ticket items as washers, refrigerators, dishwashers, large-screen TVs, and home surround-sound systems. If these are paid for out of savings, they represent a loss of interest income. If they are paid for on credit, they represent a limitation on future spending. Their operation, maintenance, and repair represent additional expense and ultimately future cost of replacement.

In considering the purchase of a consumer durable, a buyer should consider timing—certain items go on sale at certain times of the year—store, brand, rebates or other deals, and product information such as energy efficiency or safety.

Comparison shopping is an important aspect of getting a good deal on consumer durables. The internet makes it easy and cost-effective. It is also a convenient way to make purchases—as long as the buyer is dealing with a reputable site. The federal Mail Order Merchandise Rule applies to online merchants as well as catalog companies and requires that a merchant ship ordered goods within thirty days unless the buyer agrees to a delay. One important issue for consumers to check when considering an online purchase is the site's return policy if the good is unacceptable.

The features of major appliances go beyond matters of convenience. Some features can also offer financial benefits—such as those that help reduce energy usage or eliminate the need for additional appliances or other accessories.

Service contracts offered with the purchase of large items such as appliances or electronics may initially seem appealing to a consumer as a way to help minimize expenses related to future repairs, but in reality they are often a waste of money since most breakdowns tend to happen relatively soon after the purchase when a warranty would still be in effect.

Warranties

A **warranty** is a guarantee made by the manufacturer or distributor of a good that the good is as represented and will be replaced or repaired if defective. There are implied and express warranties and full and limited warranties. Goods sold "as is" carry neither an implied nor an express warranty, but all other goods carry an implied warranty and may also carry an express warranty. An **implied warranty** generally warrants the merchantability and/or fitness for purpose of a good. The former guarantees that the product is of a quality, grade, and value similar to the quality, grade, and value of similar goods, and the latter guarantees that the good is suitable for the ordinary purpose for which the seller sells it and the buyer will use it.

An **express warranty** is generally in writing and is either a full warranty or a limited warranty. A **full warranty** includes the following provisions:

- If a reasonable number of attempts at resolving the defect have not succeeded, the consumer is eligible for a replacement or a full refund.
- During the period of the warranty, the consumer cannot be charged for parts, labor, or charges to ship the good for repair.
- Whether the registration card was submitted or not does not affect the full warranty.
- The full warranty applies to subsequent owners after the original owner.
- The full warranty in no way affects the scope of the implied warranty.

A **limited warranty** is any warranty that does not include all these provisions. Extended warranties and service contracts are usually not a good buy.

TAXES

People love to hate taxes, but taxes help to pave the highways, pay air traffic controllers, provide scholarships, repair bridges, fund cancer research, offer seed money to alternative energy companies, provide security at home and abroad, construct a social safety net, and so on. Not only the federal government but also state and local governments fund their services through direct taxation. The federal government taxes earnings and wealth (and some purchases such as tires and gasoline, for example, through excise taxes); states and many municipalities tax purchases as well as earnings and property; and most states also tax wealth through an estate tax.

Payroll Deductions

Payroll deductions may be mandatory or voluntary.

Mandatory deductions include:

- Social Security Taxes, known as FICA (Federal Insurance Contributions Act):
  - *FICA-O*: Old Age Survivors Benefit
  - *FICA-M*: Medicare
- Federal income tax
- State income tax if applicable
- County/city wage tax if applicable
- State workers' compensation insurance fund if applicable

Voluntary nontax deductions may include payment for or contributions to:

- Health insurance
- Dental insurance
- Life insurance
- Long-term care insurance
- 401(k) or 403(b) pension plans

Income Tax

When you say "income tax," most people think of the federal income tax, but 43 states tax personal income, and some cities also tax income under a city wage tax provision. The types of income that are taxed are as follows:

- **Earned:** Salary, commissions, tips, bonuses
- **Investment:** Dividends from stock, interest from bonds, rent from properties
- **Passive:** Income from limited partnership or forms of limited participation in a company

Among additional types of income that are taxed are the following:

- Alimony (which is added to the payee's income and subtracted from the payer's income)
- Capital gains or losses on investments
- Jury duty pay
- Lottery and gambling winnings
- Monetary prizes and awards
- Social Security benefits (partial)
- Pensions
- Rent
- Royalties
- Travel allowance
- Unemployment compensation

While the previous list makes up a person's **gross income**, there are also certain amounts that are not included in gross income. These include exclusions such as veterans' benefits and military allowances, tax-deferred income such as contributions to traditional IRAs and Keoghs, and tax-exempt income such as the income from state and municipal bonds. These, plus such things as alimony payments, result in a person's **adjusted gross income**. This is the base amount on which people pay their federal income taxes minus further deductions. The adjusted gross income is the amount used to compute these additional deductions such as mileage for medical visits and contributions to charity.

Deductions

Taxpayers may take the standard deduction if the amount of their deductions is less than the amount of the standard deduction for any given year. The amount of the standard deduction is computed each year by the federal government. If their deductions will be greater than the amount listed as standard for any given year, taxpayers itemize.

The categories of deductions that taxpayers can itemize are:

- **State and local taxes** (typically income, real estate, and personal property, but taxpayers may deduct their state's sales tax if it is greater than their income tax)
- **Interest** (investment, mortgage, home equity line of credit)
- **Nonreimbursed medical and dental expenses**, including mileage to and from appointments
- **Charitable contributions**
- **Nonreimbursed moving expenses** related to a job relocation (if it is at least 50 miles from the current location)
- **Nonreimbursed business expenses** (such as uniforms)
- **Losses from casualty and theft**

Tax credits may also reduce a person's tax bill. These are subtracted from the taxes owed rather than subtracted from the amount on which taxes are computed. The filer computes the tax owed and then subtracts the full amount of the tax credit.

Withholding

Employees of companies receive a **W-2** form at the end of the year to verify their earned income and to file their income tax returns. The W-2 indicates the amount of taxes withheld from each paycheck. The amount of the withholding is based on the employee's **W-4** form, which indicates the number of exemptions. **Exemptions** result in deductions of a certain amount per person from adjusted gross income. The more exemptions, the less tax is withheld. A single person may take more than one exemption if the person expects to have a large tax payment when the return is filed.

Self-employed persons do not fill out W-4s nor do they receive W-2s. Instead, they file and pay estimated taxes each quarter. If they work for a number of other self-employed people or for companies, they receive **1099** forms at the end of the year from each person or company with the amount of income they received.

IRS and Audits

The Internal Revenue Service (IRS) is a bureau of the Department of the Treasury. Its purpose is to collect the proper amount of tax revenue at the least cost, serve the public by continually improving the quality of its products and services, and perform in a manner warranting the highest degree of public confidence in its integrity, efficiency, and fairness. In fiscal year 2019, the IRS collected more than $3.5 trillion in revenue, processed more than 253 million tax returns and other forms, and issued more than $452 billion in tax refunds. More than 155 million of the tax returns processed were individual income tax returns.

The IRS is organized around divisions that focus on particular constituents. There are four divisions that deal with individual taxpayers, small businesses, mid-to-large businesses, and nonprofits. These operational divisions focus on routine activities of processing tax returns, communicating with taxpayers, conducting audits, and collecting taxes.

A **tax return audit** is a review/examination of an organization's or individual's accounts and financial information to ensure information is being reported correctly, according to the tax laws, to verify the amount reported is accurate. When returns are filed, they are compared against "norms" for similar returns. The norms are developed from audits of a statistically valid random sample of returns. These returns are selected as part of the National Research Program, which the IRS conducts to update return-selection information. Following this, the return is reviewed by an experienced auditor. At this point, the return may be accepted as filed, or if, based on the auditor's experience, questionable items are noted, the auditor will identify the items noted and the return is forwarded for assignment to an examining group.

Upon examining the return, it is then reviewed by the manager. Items considered in assigning a case are factors particular to the area, such as issues pertaining to construction, farming, timber industry, etc., that have specific factors and rules that apply. Based on the review, the manager can accept the return or assign the return to an auditor. The assigned auditor again reviews the return for questionable items and either accepts it as filed or contacts the taxpayer to schedule an appointment to review the filing.

Estate and Gift Taxes

When someone in your family dies and the property of the deceased transfers to you, the federal government imposes an **estate tax** on the value of the property.

A **gift tax** is a tax imposed on the transfer of ownership of property. The federal gift tax exists for one reason: to prevent citizens from avoiding the federal estate tax by giving away their money before they die.

The gift tax is perhaps the most misunderstood of all taxes. When it comes into play, this tax is owed by the *giver* of the gift, not the recipient. The law ignores gifts of up to a certain amount per person, per year. For example, for the 2020 tax year, you may gift up to $15,000 per person. You may give to as many people as you wish without the gifts counting against you. You and your spouse together can give up to $30,000 per person, per year.

Starting in 2020, the estate and gift tax lifetime exemption is $11.58 million per individual. This means an individual can leave $11.58 million to heirs and pay no federal estate or gift tax. A married couple will be able to shield $23.16 million from federal estate and gift taxes. The federal estate and gift tax exemptions rise with inflation.

Here are some gifts that are not considered "taxable gifts" and, therefore, do not count as part of your $11.58 million lifetime total.
- Present-interest gifts
- Charitable gifts
- Gifts to a spouse
- Gifts for educational expenses
- Gifts for medical expenses
- Political organization gifts

NOTE: A present-interest gift means that the person receiving the gift has an unrestricted right to use or enjoy the gift immediately.

The tax rules and exemptions are adjusted by the IRS each year. It's important to check the IRS website and/or consult your accountant or tax planner each year.

Tax Planning/Estimating

In addition to self-employed persons, those who have income other than salaries and wages may also have to file and pay estimated taxes. There are ways to minimize a person's tax bill.

Paying Estimated Taxes

Because the federal government needs revenue to function, it requires that taxpayers with passive income estimate their whole year tax bill and pay it in quarterly installments. These include taxpayers who receive interest on bonds and savings accounts, stock dividends, royalty payments, and retirement or pension plans that are paid out as a lump sum rather than as an annuity. The government allows some leeway in figuring the tax each year. A filer isn't charged a penalty and interest if he or she makes estimated payments that total more than the previous year's tax even though the estimated payments are less than the actual tax for the current year. Also, a taxpayer will not be penalized if he or she pays estimated taxes that are 90 percent or more, but less than 100 percent, of the current year's income tax.

Tax Planning

There are a variety of legal ways that can be used to reduce taxes. Among them are the following:

- **Municipal Bond:** Tax-exempt interest under state and federal governments
- **State Bond:** Tax-exempt interest under the federal government and many states (capital gains may be taxed in certain states)
- **Primary Residence:** Tax-deductible property taxes and mortgage interest
- **Home Equity Line of Credit:** Tax-deductible interest on the loan
- **Real Estate as an Investment:** Depreciation
- **Traditional IRA, Keogh, 401(k), Tax-Deferred Annuity:** Tax-deferred investment vehicles for retirement that reduce current adjusted gross income on which taxes are computed
- **529 Savings Plan for Children's Education:** Tax-deferred investment that provides a tax credit

- **Flexible Spending Account for Health Care or Child Care:** Reduction of current adjusted gross income
- **Self-employment:** Advantages in expensing certain costs that owners would otherwise have to pay themselves, such as health insurance premiums and nonreimbursed medical bills
- **Gift Program:** Up to $15,000 (for 2020) per donor per recipient
- **Trust:** Provides income for a beneficiary who is usually at a lower tax rate than the person who used his or her own money to set up the trust
- **Tax Credits:** Variety of such credits (e.g., earned income, child care, home energy)

Progressive and Regressive Taxation

A **progressive tax structure** is one in which an individual's or family's tax liability as a fraction of income rises with income. If, for example, taxes for a family with an income of $20,000 are 20 percent of income and taxes for a family with an income of $200,000 are 30 percent of income, then the tax structure over that range of incomes is progressive. It is important to note that progressive tax can come in other forms, such as estate taxes or luxury taxes on goods. Estate taxes require higher net worth individuals to pay an additional tax on their property when they die. If the value of all the property is over a certain amount, then they most likely will be taxed.

Pros	Cons
It helps to provide a buffer against income inequality.	Those who barely break into a new tax bracket may lose their additional earnings.
It provides higher overall levels of revenue.	It creates a complicated system of bureaucracy.

Under a **regressive tax structure**, individuals and entities with low incomes pay a higher amount of that income in taxes compared to high-income earners. Rather than implementing a tax liability based on the individual's or entity's ability to pay, the government assesses tax as a percentage of the assets that the taxpayer purchases or owns. An example is state sales tax, where everyone pays the same tax rate regardless of his/her income. The most apparent advantage of this system is that it provides a positive incentive to work harder. The issue of trying to fall into a lower tax bracket is not part of the equation with the regressive system.

Other Taxes

Excise Tax

Excise taxes are taxes paid when specific purchases are made, such as gasoline. The taxes are often included in the price of the product and may be imposed by both federal and state authorities. An excise is considered an indirect tax, meaning that the producer or seller who pays the tax to the government is expected to try to recover or shift the tax by raising the price paid by the buyer.

Excise taxes usually fall into one of two types:

1. *Ad Valorem*, meaning that a fixed percentage is charged on a particular good or product; this administration of the tax is less common.
2. *Specific*, meaning that a fixed currency amount may be imposed depending on the quantity of the goods or products that are purchased; specific is the most common type.

Property Tax

Property tax is a tax that local governments impose on real estate. It is known as an ad valorem tax, which means that it is based on the value of the property. Individuals with a home or land that has a higher value pay more in property taxes, although everyone within a given municipality pays property tax at the same flat-percentage rate. Local governments use the money collected from property taxes for a number of programs. The majority of property tax revenue goes toward funding city and county governments, including meeting payroll for city employees. Property taxes also fund public schools, including local school districts and community colleges.

Sales Tax

A **sales tax** is a tax paid to a governing body for the sale of certain goods and services. Usually laws allow (or require) the seller to collect funds for the tax from the consumer at the point of purchase. When a tax on goods or services is paid to a governing body directly by a consumer, it is usually called a **use tax**. Often laws provide for the exemption of certain goods or services from sales and use taxes.

Gas Tax

A **fuel tax** (also known as a petrol or gasoline or gas tax or as a fuel duty) is an excise tax imposed on the sale of fuel. The United States federal excise tax on gasoline is 18.4 cents per gallon and 24.4 cents per gallon for diesel fuel. On average, as of July 2020, state and local taxes and fees add 29.86 cents to gasoline and 31.76 cents to diesel, for a total US average fuel tax of 48.26 cents per gallon for gas and 54.16 cents per gallon for diesel.

Tax Professionals

Any tax professional with an IRS Preparer Tax Identification Number (PTIN) is authorized to prepare federal tax returns; however, tax professionals have differing levels of skills, education, and expertise. Tax return preparers who have PTINs but are not listed in the IRS *Directory of Federal Tax Return Preparers with Credentials and Select Qualifications* may provide quality return preparation services, but, as with any decision that will affect your financial health, be sure to choose your return preparer wisely. Professional tax services range from straightforward filing to strategic long-term advice. Always ask about the preparer's education and training; it pays to know your preparer's specialty.

- **Chain or local outlet preparers** (e.g., H&R Block, Jackson Hewitt) are trained to fill out tax forms, but their experience and expertise can vary widely, and many are not full-time tax professionals; this route is best for those with uncomplicated tax issues.
- An **enrolled agent (EA)** must pass an IRS exam or have at least five years of work experience at the IRS to be licensed by the federal government; many have areas of specialty. If needed, the agent can represent taxpayers in IRS disputes.
- **Certified public accountants (CPAs)** are trained in maintaining business and financial records, but not all of them prepare tax returns. To earn the CPA designation, one must pass a four-part accounting exam. CPAs, like EAs, are qualified to face the IRS on a taxpayer's behalf. CPAs are best for those seeking a holistic tax strategy to deal with the financial issues from personal businesses, retirement, divorce, etc.
- **Certified financial planners (CFPs)** provide overall financial planning advice on savings, investments, insurance, and big-picture tax issues. Fees can be hourly, flat, or based on a percentage of your assets. Some, not all, offer tax-prep services to clients.

- **Accredited tax accountants (ATAs)** and **accredited tax preparers (ATPs)** specialize in preparing personal and business returns, as well as providing tax-planning services.
- **Tax attorneys** tend to specialize in the minutiae of the IRS tax code, particularly in the areas of trusts, estate planning, tax disputes, and business tax law. They must have a JD degree and must be admitted to the state bar. Some will prepare returns but usually at a premium cost. They also can represent clients in audit, collection, and appeals before the IRS.

INSURANCE

Insurance is about protecting against possible financial loss. Different kinds of insurance protect against different kinds of financial-related loss such as loss of life, loss of income, and loss of property. Insurance is a way to pool risk over a large number of people so that it becomes predictable. There are four strategies for risk management:

1. Risk reduction (taking preventive actions)
2. Risk avoidance (eliminating the risk)
3. Risk retention (agreeing to have some exposure to a risk)
4. Risk transfer (purchasing insurance)

Risk Management

Risk management is the continuing process to identify, analyze, evaluate, and treat loss exposures and monitor risk control and financial resources to mitigate the adverse effects of loss.

Loss may result from the following:

- Financial risks, such as cost of claims and liability judgments
- Operational risks, such as labor strikes
- Perimeter risks, including weather or political change
- Strategic risks, including management changes or loss of reputation

You face risks every day. *Risk, peril,* and *hazard* are terms used to indicate the possibility of loss. While these terms are used interchangeably in everyday life, the insurance industry distinguishes between them. A **risk** is simply the possibility of a loss, but a **peril** is a cause of loss. A **hazard** is a condition that increases the possibility of loss. For instance, fire is a peril because it causes losses, while a fireplace is a hazard because it increases the probability of loss from fire. Some things can be both a peril and a hazard.

Smoking, for instance, causes cancer and other health ailments, while also increasing the probability of such ailments. Many fundamental risks, such as hurricanes, earthquakes, or unemployment, that affect many people are generally insured by society or by the government, while particular risks that affect individuals or specific organizations, such as losses from fire or vandalism, are considered the particular responsibilities of those affected. Risk management is concerned with all loss exposures, not only the ones that can be insured. Insurance is a technique to finance some loss exposures and, therefore, a part of the broader concept of managing risk.

Life Policies

Buying life insurance has two benefits: it is a way to put aside money in savings and it provides financial security for dependents when the insured dies. In estimating whether a person needs life insurance and if so, how much, it's important to consider the person's life circumstances. A single working person in his or her mid-twenties probably doesn't need life insurance, whereas a married father in his forties with a wife who doesn't work outside the home and 3 children needs life insurance.

There are four general ways to determine life insurance needs. The **easy method** is seven years (the amount of time it is estimated to take for a family's finances to adjust after the death of a breadwinner) times 70 percent of that person's income equals the amount of life insurance required for a typical family. The **DINK method** estimates life insurance for a "dual income, no kids" couple by including funeral expenses and halving expenses like a mortgage. The **nonworking spouse method** multiplies ten years by $10,000 a year for child-related costs such as child care on the assumption that the nonworking spouse will need to go to work. The **family need method** itemizes a family's actual costs.

Types of Life Insurance

A life insurance policy may be a term policy, meaning "temporary," or a permanent policy. A term policy is bought for a certain number of years. For beneficiaries to collect, the insured must die within that period; there is no savings buildup with a term policy. There are a variety of permanent policies and each accrues cash: whole life, straight life, ordinary life, and cash value life.

Type	Format and Characteristics
Term: No Savings Buildup	**Renewable** • Renewable at the end of the term • Increased premiums as the insured ages **Multiyear Level/Straight** • Same premium for the life of the term **Convertible** • Provision that enables the insured to convert a term to a whole life policy **Decreasing: Group Mortgage Life and Credit Life** • Same premium for the life of the policy but decreasing coverage
Permanent: Savings Buildup	**Whole Life/Straight Life/Ordinary Life/Cash Value** • Same premium for the life of the policy • In comparison to term policies, higher rate in the early years of a whole life policy (term policies increase premiums with each renewal) • Increasing cash and decreasing death benefits over the life of the policy **Limited Payment Life** • Payment of premiums over a certain period, such as twenty years • Insured covered until he or she dies • Payment of death benefits on death of insured • High premium **Adjustable Life** • Premiums and coverage adjustable as the circumstances of the insured change **Universal Life** • Flexible premium payments and flexible payment schedule, that is, the insured may pay any amount at any time as well as skip payments • Policyholder receives a report identifying cost of the protection, management costs, and interest on the cash value of the policy (rate of return) **Variable and Variable-Universal** • Fixed premium • Investment of cash value in a selected portfolio of stocks, bond, money market funds • Cash value may decrease if portfolio loses value • Policyholder receives report similar to universal life • Variable-universal: flexible premiums, investment of cash value in portfolio of stocks, bonds, money market funds

Type	Format and Characteristics
Term	**Group Life** • Employer-sponsored life insurance • High premiums

Payment of death benefits may come as a lump-sum payment, limited installment payment, life income option, or payment of interest on the value. For the latter, the insurance company serves as trustee.

The face amount of a policy is its amount of death benefits. The policyholder indicates the beneficiary or beneficiaries. Other things a consumer should consider are the cash value, surrender value, premium, and dividend. Special provisions, or **riders**, can also be added to life insurance policies. These may include accelerated death benefits, accidental death benefits, cost-of-living adjustment, disability waiver of premium, grace period, guaranteed insurability option, settlement option, and survivorship life.

Property and Liability Policies

Property insurance shields people from risks to their homes, vehicles, and personal property such as furniture, electronics, and jewelry. Liability insurance protects people from losses as a result of damage done to other persons or to the property of others. Liability is responsibility under the law for the financial cost of another person's losses or injuries. The cause is usually negligence. Both homeowner's insurance and automobile insurance carry liability coverage.

Homeowner's Insurance

Homeowner's insurance covers the following:

- The main dwelling and any associated buildings on a property and also typically landscaping
- Additional living expenses for temporary housing should the property be uninhabitable for a period of time due to damage
- Personal property, such as jewelry and electronics, both at home and while the insured is traveling with the items
- Liability for injuries sustained by a guest or for damage done to property by the insured.

Personal property insurance typically places a limit on the amount of the replacement value for items. However, a personal property floater can be added to increase replacement limits; the additional coverage increases the premium.

Liability coverage includes payment for medical care for injured parties as well as legal costs for the insured should that person be sued by the injured party or the person's estate.

Typically, losses from natural disasters such as floods and earthquakes are not covered by standard homeowner's insurance, but consumers can buy **endorsements** to cover these potential risks. Endorsements are changes to the basic policy.

In determining how much insurance is needed, a homeowner needs to consider whether to purchase a policy that pays actual cash value or replacement value. The former pays out the current cost of an item minus depreciation, and the latter pays the current cost of an item without factoring in depreciation and is, therefore, more expensive to purchase.

....

TIP: Renters don't buy homeowner's insurance; they purchase renter's insurance, which covers their personal property, additional living expenses, and liability.

....

Auto Insurance

All states require drivers to carry some minimum level of auto insurance and more than half of the states have what is called a no-fault insurance system. With no-fault insurance, an injured motorist is paid by his or her own insurance company through a personal injury protection (PIP) policy regardless of who caused the accident. Payments include medical costs, lost income, and other expenses related to the accident. Depending on the state, a motorist may also need to carry residual bodily liability coverage and property damage coverage.

Three factors affect the cost of auto insurance:

1. Make and model of the vehicle
2. Rate base, also known as the rating territory
3. Driver classification

The newer and more expensive the vehicle, the higher the premium. A person who lives in a city, parks on the street, and drives 50 miles to work every day pays more than a person who lives in the suburbs, parks in her own garage, and only drives around town on the weekends. The risk for theft, damage, or an accident is greater for the first driver than the second one, so the premium is higher. A person's driving record, age, gender, and whether he or she is married or single also affect how much the person pays for car insurance.

Umbrella Policies

Homeowners' and auto insurance policies generally have limits on the amount of damages they will cover in the event of accident, injury or damage. If something happens that results in damages or losses beyond these limits, the property owner is often responsible for the difference—which could be a significant expense. This is why an umbrella policy can be a smart choice. An **umbrella policy** is an additional type of coverage that kicks in where your standard policy ends and can provide additional coverage for excess losses or expenses beyond the limits of your basic home or auto insurance policy.

Health, Disability, and Long-Term Care Policies

The goal of health, disability, and long-term care insurance is to lessen the financial burdens of providing healthcare for one's self and family.

The **Patient Protection and Affordable Care Act (PPACA)**, commonly called the **Affordable Care Act (ACA)** is a United States federal statute signed into law in 2010. The law was enacted to increase the affordability of health insurance, lower the uninsured rate in the US by expanding public and private insurance coverage, and reduce the costs of healthcare. It introduced mandates, tax subsidies, and insurance exchanges for the purchase of individual and family policies.

Health Insurance

Basic health insurance provides protection for hospital stays, surgery, and medical care. In addition to hospital expense, surgical expense, and physician expense insurance, all of which are typically bought as part of a single insurance policy, a consumer may buy major medical insurance, which pays expenses over and above the basic insurance coverage, typically up to $1 million. Major medical policies have a **deductible**—an amount that the insured must reach before benefits kick in—and a **co-payment** provision through which the insured pays some of the cost of care after the deductible has been reached. Other types of medical coverage include prescription drug coverage and dental and vision insurance.

Health insurance policies may include the following components:

- **Exclusions:** Those conditions that are not covered under a policy
- **Guaranteed Renewability:** Renewal year after year as long the premium is paid
- **Internal Limits:** Restricts the amount of payments regardless of the costs
- **Co-payment:** Insurance pays most of the charges, but the insured pays some even after the deductible has been met for the year
- **Benefit Limit:** A ceiling on the amount of costs the insurer will pay
- **Assigned Benefit:** Ability of the insured to sign payment over directly to the doctor or hospital
- **Fixed-dollar Benefit:** Pays a predetermined amount based on a per-incident or per-period basis, regardless of the actual cost of services rendered
- **Service Benefit:** Pays by services rather than by cost of services
- **Coordination of Benefits:** Enables the insured to receive benefits from primary and secondary insurance up to the total cost of the procedure or hospital stay but no more than the total

An **indemnity health insurance plan**—sometimes also called a "fee for service" plan—can be appealing to those who like freedom over their choice of healthcare providers and who don't want to deal with hassles related to referrals. This type of plan doesn't require you to be committed to one primary care doctor and also allows you to "self-refer" when you want to see a specialist. The insurance company pays you directly, paying a set amount according to their predetermined list of standard charges for specific procedures or services. You are often required to pay the healthcare provider yourself at the time services are rendered and then submit a claim for reimbursement from the insurance company.

As with other types of policies, the exact details can vary from one plan to another. Some plans place limits on pre-existing conditions, while others have no such restrictions. These plans cover a wide range of services performed by doctors, hospitals and other healthcare providers.

Health insurers include private insurance companies and health maintenance organizations (HMOs), which are also health services providers, and health services providers, such as preferred provider organizations (PPOs). The latter may be an exclusive provider organization (EPO) or a point-of-service (POS) organization. Medicare with its Medigap, Medicare Advantage, and drug prescription plans provides health coverage to those over 65 and people with certain disabilities.

HIPAA, the Health Insurance Portability and Accountability Act of 1996, ensures that workers cannot be required to requalify for health insurance when they change jobs or be charged more for health insurance than current employees. (This act is perhaps most well-known due to its sections protecting patient privacy and the security of sensitive or personal information.)

Many people receive health insurance through their employer, which can create problems if the insured person leaves that job. Individuals can then continue their health insurance coverage under the provisions of **COBRA,** the Consolidated Omnibus Budget Reconciliation Act of 1986. Under this law, many employers are required to offer terminated and laid-off workers the opportunity to continue their health insurance under the employer's plan. However, the former employee must now pay the full cost of the monthly premiums, which include the portion that was previously paid by the employer. This can result in a significant increase in the out-of-pocket cost, which often comes as a surprise to many people who plan to take advantage of the ability to continue coverage as allowed via COBRA.

Disability Insurance

Disability insurance provides income for workers who are unable to work because of a disability. What constitutes a disability depends on the insurance policy. Some policies consider a worker to be disabled if the worker cannot perform any type of work, whereas other policies consider a worker disabled if the worker cannot perform the duties of a specific job, and other policies consider a worker disabled if the worker cannot perform work-related duties or duties similar to the work for which the person was trained.

Long-Term Care Insurance

Long-term care insurance is intended to provide custodial care for those who cannot take care of themselves. Typically, policies are sold to those 60 and over who are concerned about becoming ill and disabled as they age. The benefits of a long-term care policy typically kick in when a person cannot perform some of the activities of daily living, which are bathing, dressing, being continent, eating, and being able to get around alone.

Specialty Insurance

Specialty insurance is necessary for items not covered by your ordinary homeowner's or automobile insurance. This can include, but is not limited to, flood coverage, identity theft insurance, mobile home coverage, motorcycle insurance, personal watercraft coverage, boat insurance, pet insurance, private mortgage insurance, travel insurance, title insurance, or renter's insurance.

Other types of specialty insurance include liability insurance. **Professional liability insurance** is a form of insurance designed to protect professionals and professional organizations from financial loss from their negligence. Professional liability insurance is made up of many segments and is also called errors and omissions, E&O, or malpractice insurance. Professional liability insurance is designed to protect the professional from the significant financial loss that can result from a lawsuit. Regardless of fault, litigation is costly, time consuming, and damaging to a reputation. **Malpractice insurance** is liability insurance that all physicians and most other medical providers must carry in the event that they are sued for medical malpractice. Malpractice is a medical error that results in a bad outcome and is proven to have been caused by gross negligence or deviation from the standard of care.

Specialty insurance is also available for such items as antiques and collectibles, fine art, musical instruments, and jewelry. These items may not be sufficiently covered by an individual's homeowner policy, either because of their monetary or sentimental value.

Insurance Analysis and Sources of Information

Insurance is a means of protection from financial loss. The insurance transaction involves the insured assuming a guaranteed and known relatively small loss in the form of payment to the insurer in exchange for the insurer's promise to compensate the insured in the event of a covered loss. The best way for consumers to analyze various insurance products is to conduct their own **SWOT (strengths, weaknesses, opportunities, threats) analysis** for a given product. The SWOT analysis is useful for consumers to gather information to determine the products that best suit their needs. This is created by taking a single piece of paper and dividing it into four quadrants using a single vertical and horizontal line. The top two quadrants are Strengths and Weaknesses. The bottom two quadrants are Opportunities and Threats.

Strengths	Weaknesses
List internal and external strengths in this box. Internal strengths are specific to you and your financial situation. Are you able to live within a budget? Have an emergency fund? Little to no debt? External strengths are often out of your control (such as a home purchase in a high growth real estate market). Strengths provide a solid foundation.	List weaknesses that are ongoing, foreseeable, or things that you routinely encounter. This can include personal behaviors, short-term loans, or too much debt preventing you from saving as much as you would like. Weakness can be actively addressed either by modifying certain behaviors or through improvement.
Opportunities	**Threats**
List opportunities in this box. This includes evaluating if any of your strengths and weaknesses can be leveraged into opportunities. Are there situations in the market that you can take advantage of because you are prepared? Are there foreseeable events that you could use to your financial benefit?	No one is immune to threats. Emergencies arise and an unexpected job loss or disability are threats to your financial stability. Use this box to list obstacles that are beyond your control.

INVESTMENTS

Every type of investment involves some amount of risk—and hopefully reward. Before beginning an investment program, it's important to be aware of your **risk tolerance**—the ability to endure losses in savings and investments during downturns in the economy. The lower one's risk tolerance, the safer the savings and investment vehicles should be. The higher one's risk tolerance, the riskier the savings instruments and investments can be. However, there is a **risk-return trade-off**. The lower the risk, the lower the returns, and the higher the risk, the greater the returns.

What constitutes risk? Risk factors typically are inflation, changes in interest rates, bankruptcy of a business that a person has invested in—either directly or through stocks and/or bonds—and market risk, either because of changes in the economy (systematic risk) or the behavior of investors (unsystematic). Similar risk factors can affect investments made in foreign countries.

As part of developing an investment plan, it's important to consider **asset allocation**, that is, where to save and invest one's money, and diversification within asset classes. The goal of both asset allocation and diversification is to lesson risk.

Liquid Assets

When talking about investment and risk, it's always good to consider liquid assets. As mentioned previously in this chapter, a **liquid asset** is cash or any asset that can be quickly turned into cash—personal property, stocks, short-term bonds and notes, life insurance policies with cash surrender values, and investments. A liquid asset is readily convertible to cash with little impact on its value.

Savings and Money Market Accounts and CDs

A **savings account** is one of the safest places to put money—as long as the account has less than $250,000 and the savings institution is insured by the Federal Deposit Insurance Corporation (FDIC). However, savings accounts and similar savings instruments—such as CDs, money market deposit accounts, and money market demand accounts—offer low interest rates because of this safety factor. Interest rates on money market accounts are slightly higher than on savings accounts and about the same as short-term CDs, which are lower than the rates for longer-term CDs. Brick-and-mortar and online commercial banks, credit unions, and savings and loans associations offer these savings vehicles. A person may add any amount at any time to both savings accounts and money market accounts and withdraw money at any time by using an ATM or a withdrawal slip. However, a depositor may be limited in the number of checks that can be written in any one month on a money market account. Savings accounts don't have a check-writing feature.

CDs are purchased at a set minimum deposit amount (there may not be a maximum deposit limit, depending on the financial institution) for a fixed length of time and generally at a fixed interest rate. A person cannot add to the amount in a CD, and, if the CD is redeemed before the specified period, the buyer pays a penalty.

Money market deposit and demand accounts should not be confused with money market funds, which are another form of savings and investing for people with low risk tolerance but more risk tolerance than those who invest in the other four investment vehicles. Money market funds are sold by securities brokers and mutual fund companies for $1 a share. The funds are not FDIC-insured, but the funds are principal protected, so that the value of a share does not drop below a dollar. Investors make money on the interest that their shares earn.

Rule of 72

A simple way to determine how long an investment will take to double given a fixed rate of interest is to use the **Rule of 72**: Simply divide 72 by the annual rate of return to get an estimate of the number of years it will take for the initial investment to double:

$$\text{Doubling Time (DT) interest rate} = \frac{72}{\text{interest rate}}$$

The Rule of 72 is more precise with lower rates of return such as those offered for savings accounts, CDs, and money market accounts.

Stocks, Bonds, and Stock Mutual Funds

When buying and selling stocks, bonds, and stock mutual funds, a consideration is the amount of capital gains or capital losses that the investor will have. Both will affect the investor's income taxes: losses positively and gains negatively for the investor. The exceptions are tax-exempt federal and municipal bonds.

Before venturing further into the different types of investments available, look at a few investment-related terms.

Investment Terminology

Short position (or selling short)	Occurs when an investor borrows stock from a broker with the intention of selling it at a higher price and then buying it back when the value decreases, thus making money on the difference between the price sold on the borrowed stock and the price paid to replace the stock
Call option	An agreement giving an investor the right to buy a stock, bond, or commodity for a specific price within a specified time period, made in anticipation that the asset will rise in value and the investor will make money on it
Market order	An order an investor makes to buy or sell an investment at the best available price
Buying on margin	Buying an asset by paying only a percentage of its value and borrowing the balance of the asset's cost from a broker or bank. The percentage the investor puts down is called the **margin**.
Maintenance margin requirement	The amount an investor must keep in a margin account equal to the value of assets in the account minus what the investor borrowed from the broker or bank.

| Margin call | A call from a broker to a client asking the client to increase the amount of money in his or her account for an asset bought on margin; a margin call occurs when the price of the stock falls below the initial margin requirement or percentage of the stock price invested by the client. |
| Day Trading | Buying or selling assets within a single trading day |

Stocks and Stock Mutual Funds

A **stock** is a form of equity, or ownership, in a corporation, and a **stock mutual fund** is a collection, or portfolio, of stocks from a number of companies. Stocks are classified as common or preferred; both convey voting rights on those who buy them, but preferred stockholders receive their dividends before common stockholders.

The price of a share of stock is the value of the stock. Value can rise and fall as a result of a number of factors including downturns in the economy; natural disasters and hostilities that affect production; changes in government policies, even fear of policy changes; and the financial performance of the individual company. While stocks are a risky investment, they produce higher returns than the previously discussed investment vehicles. However, some stocks are riskier than others. For example, a blue chip company like IBM® that produces quarter after quarter of strong financial results is less risky than a start-up company selling geothermal power or a tablet to compete with Apple®.

When an investor buys shares in a stock mutual fund, the person is buying shares in the company's portfolio of stocks. Buying into a stock mutual fund rather than buying individual stocks diversifies a person's risk because the person has less exposure to any one company. Mutual funds, like individual stocks, are not government insured.

Both individual stocks and stock mutual funds may pay dividends. There are two major strategies for buying and selling stocks: long-term and short-term. Long-term investing strategies include buy-and-hold, dollar-cost averaging, dividend reinvestment, and direct investment. Short-term strategies include day trading, buying on margin, selling short, trading in options, and market timing.

In determining what stocks to buy, a person should consider earning per share, price to earnings (P/E) ratio, whether or not there is a dividend, dividend yield, total return, and annualized holding per yield.

Bonds and Bond Mutual Funds

Bonds are investments in debt, not equity, and are sold by corporations and the federal and municipal governments. The company or government entity that issues the bond must pay bondholders annual interest payments for the term of the bond. At its maturity, the face value of the bond must be repaid to bondholders. The **annual rate of return** on a bond is its yield and is fixed when the bond is sold. Bonds are considered safer investments than stocks, and there are also tax advantages to owning government bonds. US Treasury bonds are exempt from state and local taxes, and municipal bonds are generally exempt from state and local taxes for residents of the state.

Like stocks, the price of bonds may rise or fall, depending on a number of factors similar to those affecting the price of stock. However, the most important factor is the credit quality of the entity that issues the bond. The stronger the company is perceived to be by a bond-rating agency—the more likely that it will make interest payments and repay the face value of the bond—the lower the interest rate. The risk is considered less. The lower the credit rating is, the riskier the investment and the higher the rate. Bond rating agencies like Moody's Investors Services rate the quality of bonds as high-grade, medium-grade, speculative, and default.

Governments—federal, state, local, and agencies—issue bonds to fund operations. Federal issues may be Treasury bills, Treasury bonds, Treasury notes, Treasury STRIPS, and Treasury inflation-indexed bonds. State and local government and agencies, such as transit authorities, secure a common type of municipal bond called a general obligation bond.

Unlike bonds, **bond mutual funds** don't promise a fixed rate of interest nor is the investor's money repaid. However, buying a bond mutual fund is safer than buying individual bonds because an investor's risk is spread across a number of corporations or government entities. It is also cheaper to buy into a bond fund than to buy individual bonds because they are typically very expensive. Bond mutual funds specialize in a category of bonds: corporate, federal government, or municipal government.

Think of mutual funds as baskets that may contain bonds, stocks, and cash equivalents. With thousands to choose from, mutual funds come in a variety of styles. They may hold a single type of asset, such as only domestic large-cap stocks, or a blend of investments, such as a balanced fund with a mix of stocks and bonds.

Equities

Equity investments involve buying and holding shares of stock in antici-pation of income (in the form of dividends) and capital gains (through an increase in the price of a stock).

Equities come in many different flavors. They represent all industries, with some based in the US and others overseas; they also come in all sizes. There are large-cap, mid-cap, and small-cap stocks. The term *cap* is short for "market capitalization," which is found by multiplying a stock's share price by the number of a company's outstanding shares.

In comparison, bonds are considered safer investments than equities. But this is not always true—it depends on the quality of the bond you buy. The riskier the bond, that is, the lower the borrower's credit quality or "rating," the higher the interest rate and the more an investor potentially has to gain, unless, of course, the borrower defaults on the bond.

It's important to become an informed investor. The following are sources that can be consulted for price-to-earnings ratios, past performance, fac-tors that may affect future performance, and similar information:

- Corporate annual, quarterly, and K-10 reports
- Investment advisers licensed by the SEC who provide guidance for a fee
- Business magazines, newspapers, and newsletters
- Financial news programs on TV and cable
- Investor subscription services accessed on the internet
- Free internet sites
- Stock exchange sites

Mutual Funds and Exchange Traded Funds

A **mutual fund** pools the assets of its investors and invests the money on behalf of the investors. The rise of mutual funds has given individual inves-tors the chance to participate in the stock market in a way not previously possible. The largest segment of the fund industry focuses on stocks, and just under half of the assets held by the industry are stocks. Within this area, investors have an extensive number of options: index funds, growth funds, sector funds, and many more. Mutual funds have costs, not just in terms of investment risk, but also in terms of fees. Like any investment, these funds have operating costs. Fees are disclosed in a fund's prospectus under the heading "Shareholder Fees."

Exchange Traded Funds (ETFs) are funds that track indexes like the NAS-DAQ-100 Index, S&P 500, and Dow Jones. When you buy shares of an ETF, you are buying shares of a portfolio that tracks the yield and return of its related index. The main difference between ETFs and other types of index funds is that ETFs do not try to outperform their corresponding index but simply replicate its performance. ETFs have been around since the early 1980s, but they've come into their own within the past 10 years.

ETFs combine the range of a diversified portfolio with the simplicity of trading a single stock. Investors can purchase ETF shares on margin, short sell shares, or hold them for the long term. The purpose of an ETF is to match a particular market index, leading to a fund management style known as passive management. Passive management is the chief distinguishing feature of ETFs, and it brings a number of advantages for investors in index funds.

Other Investment Options

Commodities, whether they are related to food, energy, or metals, are an important part of everyday life. Commodities can be an important way for investors to diversify beyond traditional stocks and bonds or to profit from commodity price movements.

It used to be that the average investor did not invest in commodities because doing so required significant amounts of time, money, and investing expertise. Today, there are a number of different routes to the commodity markets, and some of these routes make it easy for even the average investor to participate. Commodities contracts require different minimum deposits depending on the broker, and the value of an account will increase or decrease with the value of the contract. If the value of the contract goes down, the investor will be subject to a **margin call** and will be required to place more money into an account to keep the position open. Small price movements can mean huge returns or losses, and a futures account can be wiped out or doubled in a matter of minutes. Most futures contracts also have options associated with them. **Options** on futures contracts still allow one to invest in the futures contract, but they limit one's loss to the cost of the option. Options are derivatives and usually do not move point-for-point with the futures contract.

Historically, gold and silver have been popular investments for individual investors. For thousands of years, gold and silver have been used as a basis for currency value, either minted into coins or used to back currency value. When a currency is backed by gold, for example, or is "on the gold standard," there should be a direct relationship between the value of the currency and the value of the gold. In times of inflation or deflation, investors worry that the value or purchasing power of currency will change. They may invest in gold or silver as a more stable store of wealth than the currency that is supposed to represent the metal; in other words, if investors lose faith in the currency that represents the gold, they may trade their money for the gold. Most currencies used today are not backed by a precious metal but by the productivity and soundness of the economy that issues them. For example, the value of the US dollar is not related to the value of an ounce of gold but to the value of the US economy.

Investors who want to add a real estate investment to their portfolio more often make an **indirect investment**. That is, they buy shares in an entity or group that owns and manages property. For example, they may become limited partners in a real estate syndicate. A **syndicate** is a group created to buy and manage commercial property such as an apartment, office building, or shopping mall. The syndicate may be structured as a corporation or, more commonly, as a limited partnership. In a limited partnership, there is a general partner and limited partners. The general partner manages the entity, while the limited partners invest in partnership shares.

Sources of Information

In many financial decisions, identifying and evaluating risk is difficult. The best ways to consider risk are to gather information based on your experience and the experiences of others and to use financial planning information sources. Despite heavy regulation, the finance industry has its share of unethical, and sometimes illegal, operators. Investors must learn to identify a source they can understand and trust before they invest.

The media, including newspapers and other publications, provide current news on financial events that an investor can use to research market trends and opportunities. Financial institutions provide advice on investments that they offer. If you shop around and ask questions, you can compare different products from a range of providers. Institutions with this information include any company that provides these investment products, such as banks, building societies, credit unions, and insurance companies.

A number of people who work in the industry can also help you make informed investment decisions. In addition to investment advisers who work for financial institutions, you can obtain advice about shares from stockbrokers and other kinds of advice from independent financial planners. A responsible adviser will gather as much information about you as possible in order to ascertain which investment may suit you and your situation. They should determine your financial position by taking into account your income, assets, debts, and financial commitments and then speak to you directly about your investment objectives. They should also take into account your personality and assess your risk tolerance.

Time Value of Money

Time value of money is the increase in an amount of money as a result of interest earned on it. It is the future value of money calculated at a certain rate of interest over a certain period of time. Analyzing yield—percentage return on investment—and time period is important in determining where to save and invest. The formula for annual compounding is $FV = PV(1 + i)$, where i equals interest and n equals the number of years.

What if a person has a certain goal in mind, such as having $20,000 for a down payment for a condominium in four years? To determine how much to invest to achieve a certain amount, the person needs to work backwards to find the present value of money; that is, the current value for a future amount based on a certain rate of interest and certain period of time. The process is called **discounting**, and the formula is $PV = FV / (1 + i)$, where i equals interest and n equals the number of years.

Annual Percentage Rate (APR) is an attempt to standardize the calculation of the cost of borrowing to make meaningful comparisons. APR is an annualized rate that can also include other costs of borrowing in addition to the interest charges. APR does NOT reflect compounding of interest within each year. It's easy to confuse APR and the interest rate, but each element has a distinct role.

- **Nominal interest rate:** The amount that is charged on your balance in a given period of time
- **Nominal APR:** The nominal interest rate multiplied by the number of periods in a year
- **Effective interest rate:** Expressed annually, it accounts for compounding, but not fees.
- **Effective APR:** This typically accounts for both compounding interest and any fees charged on the loan.

The interest rate is the rate used to calculate the amount of interest charged each period. When multiplied by the number of periods in the year, you get the nominal APR. The effective interest rate includes compounding, while the effective APR includes both compounding and fees.

Weighing **opportunity cost** is also part of determining how much to save and invest and where. Opportunity cost is the answer to the question: What will a person give up now in order to have more later? In terms of investments, opportunity cost may also be gauged as amount of risk versus amount of return.

Asset/Portfolio Allocation

Asset allocation involves dividing an investment portfolio among different asset categories, such as stocks, bonds, and cash. The process of determining which mix of assets to hold in a portfolio is a personal one. The asset allocation that works best for an investor at any given point in his/her life will depend largely on time horizon and ability to tolerate risk.

There is no one-size-fits-all asset allocation model. What is good for one investor might not be good for another due to the current size of one's nest egg, risk tolerance, years until retirement, and other considerations. However, one thing that every investor should do is rebalance his/her portfolio to maintain the desired allocation; this is because over time an allocation will likely change.

Ultimately, the objective of a good asset allocation plan is to develop an investment portfolio that will help an investor reach his/her financial objectives with a comfortable degree of risk. A well-diversified plan will not outperform the top asset class in any given year, but over time it may be one of the most effective ways to realize one's long-term goals. Asset allocation helps investors stay in control of their financial plan by tailoring investments to fit individual goals and tolerance for risk.

The most common reason for an asset allocation is a change in an investor's time horizon; as an investor gets closer to his/her investment goal, changes to asset allocation will likely be needed. For example, most people investing for retirement hold fewer stocks and more bonds and cash equivalents as they get closer to their retirement age.

RETIREMENT AND ESTATE PLANNING

Retirement planning involves reviewing assets and living expenses. The increasing average life expectancy, the declining power of the dollar over time because of inflation, and the inadequacy of Social Security and pensions to cover living expenses are three major reasons to begin planning and saving for retirement early. Among the assets to consider in retirement planning are housing and investments, including life insurance and annuities. Downsizing living space and housing expenses has become a goal of many baby-boomers as they move into retirement.

Terminology

Before we discuss the options and strategies for retirement planning, let's define a few key terms.

Vesting

Vesting refers to whether or not the money that has been set aside for an individual contributor in a retirement plan can be kept by the individual if employment is terminated. Vested benefits are those to which the investor has an absolute right even if he/she resigns or is terminated. *Vesting* is a term used in the Employee Retirement Income Security Act (ERISA). ERISA protects the rights of employees to receive certain promised benefits, including pension benefits and income from profit-sharing plans, once they have worked at a job for a certain period of time.

Maturity

Maturity is the date on which the life of a transaction or financial instrument ends, after which it must either be renewed or it will cease to exist.

Rollovers

A **rollover** is a method of moving money from one account to another account. Typically, the term rollover is used to describe what happens with retirement accounts when they are moved from one account to another account that falls under the same tax category, all without incurring IRS penalties or taxes. A tax-deferred rollover occurs when one withdraws cash or assets from one eligible retirement plan and contributes them to another eligible retirement plan within sixty days. When handled correctly, completing a rollover is the best way to move money among retirement accounts.

An investor generally cannot make more than one rollover from the same IRA within a one-year period. Also, an investor cannot make a rollover during this one-year period from the IRA to which the distribution was rolled over. Beginning January 1, 2015, an investor can make only one rollover from an IRA to another (or the same) IRA in any twelve-month period, regardless of the number of IRAs the investor owns.

The one-per-year limit does not apply to:

- Rollovers from traditional IRAs to Roth IRAs (conversions)
- Trustee-to-trustee transfers to another IRA
- IRA-to-plan rollovers
- Plan-to-IRA rollovers
- Plan-to-plan rollovers

Qualified Retirement Accounts

There are a variety of ways to fund retirement. A person has no control over some, that is, whether the companies he or she works for during a career have pension plans and what type. There are other methods of retirement funding that a person can choose to invest in, such as a 401(k) plan and an IRA.

Company Pension Plans

Company pension plans are either **defined benefit or defined contribution** plans. With a defined benefit plan, the company states the monthly benefit that retirees will receive. An amount of money is invested annually for each employee to generate enough dividends and interest to pay the stipulated benefits when the employee retires. The Pension Benefit Guaranty Corporation (PBGC) insures defined benefit plans in case the company goes bankrupt.

With a defined contribution plan, a company does not specify the amount of monthly benefits. The company contributes a certain amount of money into each employee's investment account with a brokerage firm. The amount of benefits depends on how well the investments perform. When employees retire, they can convert the amount in the account to an annuity.

To receive benefits, an employee must vest in the pension plan, that is, work for the company for a certain period of time in order to be eligible for pension benefits. However, under the ERISA, an employee is vested in his or her own contributions immediately. The Pension Protection Act of 2006 set up a schedule of vesting for employer contributions. Retirement age for company plans is typically 65; however, employees typically can retire with "55 and 10," that is, at age 55 with 10 years of service.

In addition to monetary benefits, company pension plans may also include medical and disability benefits. Some have a survivorship benefit as well.

Additional Company Retirement Plans

Pension plans are becoming more rare. Instead, companies are offering one of the following:

- **401(k) for Private Companies, 403(b) for Nonprofits, and 457 for Public Institutions:** Contributions taken from salary/wages; tax-deferred; employers may contribute depending on how the plan is set up
- **Profit-Sharing:** Similar to a defined contribution plan, though the company only contributes in years when there is a profit
- **Employee Stock Option Plan (ESOP):** Employer's contributions in company stock
- **Simplified Employee Pension Plan (SEP):** Immediate vesting; may be set up as a pension plan or a tax-deferred IRA; also used by self-employed persons
- **Savings Incentive Match Plan for Employees (SIMPLE):** Either an IRA or 401(k); company matches employees' contributions

An ESOP is problematic if employees tie up all or most of their retirement funding in their company's stock. If the company's stock value and earnings fall either because of issues with the company or because of a decline in its market sector or in the general economy, retirees can find their income severely curtailed.

Individual Retirement Plans (IRAs)

In addition to company-sponsored retirement plans, there are ways that individuals may save and invest for retirement.

- **Individual Retirement Account (IRA):** Tax deferred until the income is withdrawn; penalties for early withdrawal, that is, prior to age 59½, except for large medical expenses, higher education costs, and first-time homebuyers; certain income and contribution restrictions apply

- **Roth IRA:** Contribution dollars are post-tax; income at the time of withdrawal is not taxed as long as the account has been in existence for at least five years and the person is 59½; certain contribution restrictions
- **Rollover IRA:** Consolidated contributions from several retirement plans; may occur as a person moves from company to company
- **Spousal IRA:** IRA for a spouse who is not employed outside of the home
- **Keogh (HR-10) Plan:** For contributions from self-employment income only
- **Annuity:** Plan purchased from an insurance company to provide income during retirement; ends only with the person's death

There are several types of annuities: **fixed**, although the insurance company may change the rate annually, and **variable**, for which the rate of return varies with the performance of the funds in which the insurance company invests. An annuity may also be **immediate**, which begins to pay income immediately, or **deferred**, which begins paying at some later date. Income is tax-deferred until an annuity begins to pay it out.

Social Security Benefits

Social Security covers almost 100 percent of US workers. Exceptions are federal government employees, survivors of those killed during active military duty who are covered under the Department of Veterans Administration, and employees covered under the Railroad Retirement System. To be eligible for Social Security, a worker must work forty quarters and earn a minimum amount, which is adjusted upward each year to keep pace with increases in wages nationwide. A person's actual amount of benefits is based on the person's actual earnings up to the contribution ceiling for each year.

A person can begin collecting Social Security at age 62, but benefits are reduced by about 25 percent. Beginning with those born between 1943 and 1954, full retirement age is 66. After 1954, full retirement age edges up incrementally (2 months for each year) to 67 for those born in 1960 and later. In addition to the retiree, the person's family may also be eligible to receive Social Security benefits under certain conditions: a spouse if 62 or older, a spouse if under 62 but taking care of the retiree's child under age 16, a former spouse age 62 or older and children up to age 18, children ages 18 and 19 if they are full-time high school students, and children over 18 with disabilities. Whether a spouse opts to take his or her own benefits or the benefits of the retiree should depend on which spouse will receive the greater benefit.

If a person begins receiving Social Security benefits before full-retirement age and continues to work, benefits are reduced by $1 for every $2 that the person receives over a certain amount. Once a person attains full-retirement age, there is no retirement test of earnings. Up to 85 percent of Social Security benefits can be taxed, depending on a recipient's other income. Depending on the rate of inflation, the government calculates an annual cost-of-living adjustment.

Wills, Trusts, and Estate Planning

Estate planning isn't just a matter of making sure that a person leaves directions for disposition of his or her assets after death. It's also a matter of building up those assets during one's lifetime. Financial planning is part of a life plan, and planning for the transfer of those assets is part of a death plan.

Wills

Whether a person is part of a married or nontraditional couple or single, everyone needs a written will. Dying without a valid will is called dying intestate. There are various formats for wills, but in some states, a person may be required to leave one half of his or her assets to the surviving spouse:

- **Simple Will:** Leaves everything to a spouse
- **Traditional Marital Share Will:** Leaves half the adjusted gross estate to a spouse and the other half in trust to the spouse or to children or others
- **Exemption Trust Will:** Leaves all but a small amount to a spouse; the remainder is put in trust for the spouse
- **Stated Dollar Amount Will:** Leaves certain amounts to a spouse and to other heirs (leaving a percentage rather than an amount is a safer strategy because the value of an estate may rise or fall depending on economic factors)

Under a simple will, estate taxes are paid at the time of the death of the person whose will is being probated. Under a traditional marital share, half the taxes are paid on the death of the person and half at the death of the spouse. The exemption trust results in almost no tax payment for the estate or at the time of the death of spouse. Taxes may vary under a stated dollar amount depending on how much is left to a spouse.

If there is no requirement to leave half an estate to the spouse or the spouse has predeceased, there are two ways that an estate may be divided: **per capita** and **per stirpes**. The former divides the assets into equal shares, and the latter divides everything equally among the branches of a family. An important part of writing a will is selecting the executor who will see that the terms of the will are carried out and also that all debts are paid and taxes are filed and paid, if required. If a person dies intestate, the court appoints an executor. Those with children or spouses unable to care for themselves or anyone else who is a dependent would also have to name a guardian to handle affairs for the person or persons.

Trusts and Estates

A **trust** is a legal arrangement by which one party holds the rights to property for the benefit of another party or parties. A **testamentary trust** is one that comes into existence upon the death of the owner of the property and is typically used for the support of dependent children; minor children cannot inherit property directly. A **living trust**, formally known as an *inter vivos* trust, is set up during the lifetime of the owner of the assets and, as a result, does not require probate. Living trusts are subject to estate taxes if they are revocable trusts but not if they are irrevocable. A **life insurance trust** is a type of living trust that is funded by the proceeds of a person's life insurance upon the person's death. A trust can also be established by a person for the person's own benefit during his or her lifetime. It is a way to ensure that a person will be taken care of should he or she no longer be able to do so. Trusts can also be set up to provide for the support of a spouse or other dependents, transfer assets without going through probate, reduce estate taxes, and pay estate taxes.

An **estate** is the sum total of all of a person's assets. How an estate is taxed depends on whether the decedent was married and lived in a community property state or not. In a community property state, each spouse owns half of the assets. In a noncommunity state, individual ownership is recognized, though joint ownership is typical. **Joint ownership** may be classified as joint ownership with a right of survivorship, tenants in common, and tenancy by entirety. Each has its own tax consequences. Joint ownership with right of survivorship and tenancy by entirety result in no estate tax at the death of the first spouse (and no need to pass through probate court). Tenancy in common also results in no estate tax for a spouse, but if the joint owners are not married, for example, a parent and child, there would be a tax liability. Upon the death of a tenant in common, the estate must pass through probate court.

Life insurance proceeds are not included in an estate if the policy has been assigned to a beneficiary or a trust. Any death benefits from company pensions, profit-sharing, and Keogh plans are not part of a person's taxable estate unless the estate is the payee.

Tax-Deferred Annuities

An **annuity** is a contract between an individual and an insurance company that provides the individual with tax-deferred accumulation and an option to receive a lump sum or fixed-periodic payments starting on a specific date.

An annuity can offer benefits such as:

- Control over when the individual pays taxes by timing distributions
- Unlimited contributions
- Option of guaranteed income for life
- A cost of living adjustment (COLA) that ensures payouts increase in order to offset the effects of inflation
- A death benefit that passes account value to beneficiaries, which may avoid probate but is not tax-free

The federal government levies a federal estate tax, sometimes called a "death tax," on estates in excess of a certain amount. That amount has varied over the last decade from $1.5 million to $11.58 million depending on certain temporary tax provisions. Gifting children $15,000 a year ($30,000 for a married couple) is one way to transfer wealth from one generation to the next without incurring taxes. In addition to federal estate taxes, states also levy estate taxes. Rates vary from state to state. States also levy inheritance taxes on the heirs of a decedent's estate. Tax rates, exemptions, and other provisions vary from state to state. In general, the larger the estate and the greater the distance between decedent and heir, the higher the inheritance tax rate. Gifting during one's lifetime is one way to avoid having an heir pay an inheritance tax. The federal government doesn't levy an inheritance tax.

SUMMING IT UP

- Financial goals may be **short-term**, **medium-term**, or **long-term**. They can also be categorized as **consumable-product**, **durable-product**, and **intangible-product goals**. Financial goals change in importance as a person moves through each stage of the life cycle.
- Once financial goals are set, it's important to establish a **budget** to achieve those goals.

- A **cash flow statement** shows inflow and outflow of money and is useful in planning a household budget. A **balance sheet** lists assets minus liabilities to show an individual's or family's net worth.
- **Cash management** is a way to have cash, or the equivalent, handy for regular purchases and emergencies.
- The **time value of money** is the increase in the amount of money as a result of interest earned on it. It is, in other words, the future value of money calculated at a certain rate of interest over a certain period of time.
  - Two other important concepts are the **present value of money** and **opportunity cost**. The former is the current value of money needed to generate a future amount based on a certain rate of interest and a certain period of time. The latter is what a person gives up in order to gain something else.
- **Credit** is the promise to pay later for the use of something now.
  - **Advantages of using credit** include convenience, the ability to consume more than possible based on income, as a hedge against inflation, and for emergencies.
  - **Disadvantages of using credit** are the temptation to spend more than a person has, the consequences of overspending, the cost of credit, and limitations on future spending power because of the cost of credit for past purchases.
  - There are three types of credit: installment sales credit, installment cash credit, and **single lump-sum credit**. Repayment for the first two is in regular amounts over a period of time.
- The five Cs of creditworthiness are **character**, **capacity**, **capital**, **collateral**, and **conditions**. A creditor checks an applicant's credit score, known as a **FICO score**, which considers length of credit history, on-time payment history, current amounts owed, types of credit in the credit history, and inquiries from new credit sources.
- There are two forms of personal bankruptcy: **Chapter 7, known as straight bankruptcy**, and **Chapter 13, known as the wage-earner plan**. Filing for bankruptcy stays on a personal financial record for seven or ten years and can affect the ability to qualify for credit or a job and to buy insurance.
- A basic question for many when faced with obtaining a car is whether to buy or lease. A comparison can be made based on initial costs, monthly payments, and final expenses to pay off the lease.
  - In **evaluating leases**, a consumer should note the capitalized cost, interest rate, amount of monthly payments, number of monthly payments, residual value of the vehicle at turn-in time, and early lease-termination fee.

- ⊛ If **deciding to buy**, a consumer faces the choice: new or used. The price of a used car is determined by mileage, condition, features and options, and demand in the marketplace for the make and model.
- ⊛ Whether new or used, a car owner must be able to finance costs of ownership and costs of operation.
- The **advantages of renting housing** are mobility, little or no personal or financial responsibility for maintenance or repairs, and the lower initial cost of paying only a security deposit. The **disadvantages** are inability to derive financial benefits from ownership (tax deductions, increasing equity stake), the likelihood of rent increases over time, and lease restrictions on use of the rental property.
- **The advantages of buying housing** include tax deductions for mortgage interest and property taxes, capital gain that is probably not taxable because of tax adjustments, and fewer restrictions on how the property can be used. **Disadvantages** are limited mobility, maintenance and repair costs, high initial costs, and loss of potential interest earned on money used for the down payment and closing costs.
- The larger the down payment on a home, the lower the monthly payments. The longer the term of the mortgage, the higher the interest rate. Depending on the down payment, a lender may require private mortgage insurance.
- Most mortgages are **conventional mortgages** and are for terms of thirty, twenty, or fifteen years. There are also a variety of other types of mortgages, including **adjustable rate**, **interest-only**, and **convertible**.
- **Payroll deductions** may be mandatory or voluntary, depending on whether they are tax or nontax deductions from wages.
- Taxpayers may take the **standard deduction** when reporting their income or itemize their deductions if they are higher than the standard deduction in any given year.
- There are a variety of legal ways to reduce taxes, which is known as **tax avoidance**.
- **Life insurance policies** may be **term policies** or **whole life**. The latter includes a savings component and has a number of formats. Life insurance policies have a face value, which is the amount of death benefits.
- **Property insurance** shields people from risks to their homes, vehicles, and personal property such as furniture, electronics, and jewelry. **Liability insurance** protects people from losses as a result of damage done to other persons or to the property of others. Both homeowner's and auto insurance may include both components.

- **Basic health insurance** provides protection for hospital stays, surgery, and medical care. **Major medical insurance** pays expenses over and above the basic insurance coverage, typically up to $1 million. The Affordable Care Act, which became law in 2010, affects the rules and requirements surrounding health insurance in the United States.
- **Disability insurance** provides income for workers who are unable to work because of a disability. What constitutes a disability depends on the insurance policy.
- **Investments** involve risk, but the least risky are savings accounts, money market deposit/money market demand accounts, money market funds, and certificates of deposit. Individual stocks and bonds are riskier than stock mutual funds and bond mutual funds, because with the latter two, risk is spread over more companies.
- There are a variety of ways to fund retirement through **employer-sponsored plans**:
    ◦ Company pension plans, which may be defined benefit or defined contribution plans: 401(k), 403(b), and 457 plans
    ◦ Profit-sharing plan
    ◦ Employee Stock Option Plan (ESOP)
    ◦ Simplified Employee Pension Plan (SEP)
    ◦ Savings Incentive Match Plan for Employees (SIMPLE)
- Individuals can also establish retirement plans through **Individual Retirement Account (IRA), Roth IRA, rollover IRA, spousal IRA, Keogh (HR-10) Plan**, and **annuity**, which may be fixed or variable and immediate or deferred.
- **Estate planning** involves writing a will. Depending on the state, a person may be required to leave at least half of his or her estate to the spouse.
    ◦ **Trusts** may be testamentary or living, also known as *inter vivos*. A living trust may be revocable or irrevocable.
    ◦ The federal government levies a **federal estate tax** on estates in excess of a certain amount. States also levy estate taxes and some also tax the heirs.

Chapter 4

Personal Finance Post-Test

POST-TEST ANSWER SHEET

1. Ⓐ Ⓑ Ⓒ Ⓓ	18. Ⓐ Ⓑ Ⓒ Ⓓ	35. Ⓐ Ⓑ Ⓒ Ⓓ
2. Ⓐ Ⓑ Ⓒ Ⓓ	19. Ⓐ Ⓑ Ⓒ Ⓓ	36. Ⓐ Ⓑ Ⓒ Ⓓ
3. Ⓐ Ⓑ Ⓒ Ⓓ	20. Ⓐ Ⓑ Ⓒ Ⓓ	37. Ⓐ Ⓑ Ⓒ Ⓓ
4. Ⓐ Ⓑ Ⓒ Ⓓ	21. Ⓐ Ⓑ Ⓒ Ⓓ	38. Ⓐ Ⓑ Ⓒ Ⓓ
5. Ⓐ Ⓑ Ⓒ Ⓓ	22. Ⓐ Ⓑ Ⓒ Ⓓ	39. Ⓐ Ⓑ Ⓒ Ⓓ
6. Ⓐ Ⓑ Ⓒ Ⓓ	23. Ⓐ Ⓑ Ⓒ Ⓓ	40. Ⓐ Ⓑ Ⓒ Ⓓ
7. Ⓐ Ⓑ Ⓒ Ⓓ	24. Ⓐ Ⓑ Ⓒ Ⓓ	41. Ⓐ Ⓑ Ⓒ Ⓓ
8. Ⓐ Ⓑ Ⓒ Ⓓ	25. Ⓐ Ⓑ Ⓒ Ⓓ	42. Ⓐ Ⓑ Ⓒ Ⓓ
9. Ⓐ Ⓑ Ⓒ Ⓓ	26. Ⓐ Ⓑ Ⓒ Ⓓ	43. Ⓐ Ⓑ Ⓒ Ⓓ
10. Ⓐ Ⓑ Ⓒ Ⓓ	27. Ⓐ Ⓑ Ⓒ Ⓓ	44. Ⓐ Ⓑ Ⓒ Ⓓ
11. Ⓐ Ⓑ Ⓒ Ⓓ	28. Ⓐ Ⓑ Ⓒ Ⓓ	45. Ⓐ Ⓑ Ⓒ Ⓓ
12. Ⓐ Ⓑ Ⓒ Ⓓ	29. Ⓐ Ⓑ Ⓒ Ⓓ	46. Ⓐ Ⓑ Ⓒ Ⓓ
13. Ⓐ Ⓑ Ⓒ Ⓓ	30. Ⓐ Ⓑ Ⓒ Ⓓ	47. Ⓐ Ⓑ Ⓒ Ⓓ
14. Ⓐ Ⓑ Ⓒ Ⓓ	31. Ⓐ Ⓑ Ⓒ Ⓓ	48. Ⓐ Ⓑ Ⓒ Ⓓ
15. Ⓐ Ⓑ Ⓒ Ⓓ	32. Ⓐ Ⓑ Ⓒ Ⓓ	49. Ⓐ Ⓑ Ⓒ Ⓓ
16. Ⓐ Ⓑ Ⓒ Ⓓ	33. Ⓐ Ⓑ Ⓒ Ⓓ	50. Ⓐ Ⓑ Ⓒ Ⓓ
17. Ⓐ Ⓑ Ⓒ Ⓓ	34. Ⓐ Ⓑ Ⓒ Ⓓ	51. Ⓐ Ⓑ Ⓒ Ⓓ

52. Ⓐ Ⓑ Ⓒ Ⓓ   55. Ⓐ Ⓑ Ⓒ Ⓓ   58. Ⓐ Ⓑ Ⓒ Ⓓ

53. Ⓐ Ⓑ Ⓒ Ⓓ   56. Ⓐ Ⓑ Ⓒ Ⓓ   59. Ⓐ Ⓑ Ⓒ Ⓓ

54. Ⓐ Ⓑ Ⓒ Ⓓ   57. Ⓐ Ⓑ Ⓒ Ⓓ   60. Ⓐ Ⓑ Ⓒ Ⓓ

PERSONAL FINANCE POST-TEST
72 minutes—60 questions

Directions: Carefully read each of the following 60 questions. Choose the best answer to each question and fill in the corresponding circle on the answer sheet. The Answer Key and Explanations can be found following this post-test.

---

1. If a homebuyer has less than 20 percent for a down payment, the homebuyer will

   A. need to buy mortgage insurance.
   B. have to apply for an FHA mortgage.
   C. be turned down by the VA.
   D. need to come up with 5 percent more of the down payment.

2. One difference between CDs and savings accounts and money markets is that

   A. the interest rate on a CD varies over time, whereas the interest rate on a savings account or a money market does not.
   B. money cannot be added to a CD over time, whereas money can be added to a savings account or money market.
   C. a CD is not FDIC-insured, but the other two are.
   D. a CD is a good savings vehicle for someone with a low tolerance for risk, but the other two are not.

3. The future value of money is

   A. the amount a given amount of money will be worth in the future when adjusted for inflation
   B. the increase in an amount of money including interest earned over time.
   C. the value of money in today's marketplace.
   D. money earned as profit on an investment.

4. Which of the following does NOT impact vested benefits?

   A. Length of time worked for an employer
   B. Regulations outlined in Employee Retirement Income Security Act
   C. Amount of notice an employee gives when resigning position
   D. Specific type of benefit involved

5. Which of the following does NOT reduce current tax obligations?

A. Roth IRA
B. Traditional IRA
C. Spousal IRA
D. SEP

6. A Chapter 13 bankruptcy remains on a person's credit report for

A. five years.
B. seven years.
C. eight years.
D. ten years.

7. Jason graduated from college in June. He started a job later that month that is paying him an average salary for a new employee in his field. He's sharing an apartment with three roommates and has $30,000 in student loans to pay off. What should his immediate financial goal be?

A. Paying off his student loans as fast possible
B. Setting up a retirement plan
C. Buying life insurance
D. Setting up a six-month emergency fund

8. In calculating income tax, when are tax credits applied in the process?

A. Before calculating adjusted gross income
B. When calculating gross income
C. After calculating the income tax owed
D. Before standard deductions and any exemptions are taken

9. Renting a home instead of buying would generally be a wise financial move for someone who

A. is seeking a long-term investment.
B. wants the freedom to use the property however they wish, including leasing it for income.
C. is interested in tax deductions.
D. is likely to move within a year or two.

10. In terms of benefits, a term life policy provides

 A. death benefits, can be borrowed against, and cash if it is a policy that pays dividends.
 B. death benefits and cash if it is a policy that pays dividends.
 C. death benefits and can be borrowed against.
 D. death benefits only.

11. A disadvantage for homebuyers to owning any type of housing is the potential

 A. for disagreements over association rules.
 B. decline in housing prices.
 C. lack of privacy.
 D. assessment fees.

12. The full retirement age for the purpose of receiving Social Security for those born in 1945 is

 A. $62\frac{1}{2}$
 B. 65.
 C. 66.
 D. 67.

13. The benefit from a resource that a person gives up in choosing one option over another is called its

 A. opportunity cost.
 B. lost opportunity.
 C. alternative.
 D. trade-off.

14. In buying a refrigerator, a consumer would most likely consider which of the following first?

 A. Volume discount
 B. Features
 C. Trade-in value
 D. Service contract

15. A liquid asset is one that

    A. can be quickly converted to cash.

    B. guarantees an attractive profit potential.

    C. involves significant red tape or a cumbersome management process.

    D. cannot be accessed or withdrawn for a year or more.

16. Which of the following allows the fastest access to cash with no penalty for withdrawal?

    A. Regular checking account

    B. Certificate of deposit

    C. Series EE bond

    D. Stocks

17. Jake wants to improve his credit score. Which of the following will help him to do this?

    A. Take out several new credit cards

    B. Buy several major appliances using store credit

    C. Open a savings account and make regular deposits each time he is paid

    D. Check his credit score regularly

18. Which of these is a mandatory payroll deduction?

    A. Social Security taxes

    B. 401(k) or 403(b) pension plans

    C. Long-term care insurance

    D. Health insurance

19. Which of the following is both a health insurer and a health services provider?

    A. Health maintenance organization

    B. Preferred provider organization

    C. Point-of-service plan

    D. Fee-for-service

20. Which of the following is a typical rider to a life insurance policy?

    A. Grace period

    B. Automatic premium clause

    C. Cost-of-living protection

    D. Policy loan provision

21. Nadja was comparing credit cards and decided not to take the card from Acme Bank. Which of the following features signaled to Nadja that Acme's card was not a good choice?

A. The grace period was 21 days.
B. Interest was charged from the day that a purchase was made.
C. The card offered buyer protection for purchases.
D. The annual fee was waived because it was a special offer.

22. Reduction of the principal borrowed over the life of a mortgage is called

A. RESPA.
B. rate cap.
C. escrow accounting.
D. amortization.

23. Which of the following is an accurate statement about payroll deductions?

A. All payroll deductions are mandatory.
B. FICA taxes include Old Age Survivors Benefit and Medicare.
C. IRA contributions are taken directly as payroll deductions.
D. A worker can have the premium for a non-company–sponsored life insurance policy deducted from his or her paycheck.

24. Under which of the following programs can an employee who has been terminated or laid off continue health insurance for a period of time?

A. HIPAA
B. Medigap
C. COBRA
D. COB

25. Any debt that must be paid within a year is a

A. current liability.
B. noncurrent liability.
C. flexible expense.
D. dissavings.

26. When making a major purchase such as a computer or appliance, you can benefit financially by

   A. buying on credit.
   B. comparison shopping.
   C. paying for the purchase with money withdrawn from a CD or interest-bearing savings account.
   D. opting for the extra service plan.

27. Which of the following is a reason that a person may withdraw money from an IRA before age $59\frac{1}{2}$ without incurring a penalty?

   A. To buy a car
   B. To pay for a college education
   C. To purchase a vacation home
   D. For a large-scale home renovation

28. An indemnity health insurance policy is NOT ideal because it

   A. pays only a specified amount regardless of actual costs.
   B. does not cover pre-existing conditions.
   C. will not pay you directly, only the healthcare provider.
   D. pays only for regular nonsurgical doctors' services.

29. Sal and Joanna decided against taking out an umbrella policy. This was an unwise decision because an umbrella policy

   A. covers a home office, and Joanna runs a business out of their house.
   B. protects against flood damage, and they live in a floodplain.
   C. would have provided minimal health insurance as well as homeowner's and auto insurance.
   D. extends liability coverage over and above the limits in homeowner's and auto insurance policies.

30. A disadvantage of a regressive tax structure is that

   A. it is complicated to calculate and implement.
   B. those who move up just slightly into a higher tax bracket can suffer a financial penalty.
   C. lower-income people pay a proportionally higher amount of taxes than those with a higher income.
   D. it offers little motivation to work hard or increase one's income.

31. Asset allocation involves

    A. working toward financial goals with a comfortable level of risk.

    B. a standard formula that dictates how assets should always be divided.

    C. committing to a specific plan indefinitely without deviations or changes.

    D. dividing up valuables and giving them away to friends and family.

32. Estimated taxes are paid

    A. weekly.

    B. monthly.

    C. quarterly.

    D. twice a year.

33. Stock mutual funds can be a smart investment choice because they

    A. can help minimize overall risk.

    B. are insured by the federal government.

    C. have a fixed rate of return so it is easy to calculate what the profit will be.

    D. enable an investor to select specific companies to invest in.

34. An agency like Moody's Investors Services can

    A. guide an entity in repairing or improving their credit score.

    B. help investors determine bonds with the least amount of risk.

    C. set the price of stocks and bonds.

    D. provide individual investors with financial management or accounting services.

35. Alexis believes that buying used cars makes more financial sense than buying new cars. He bases his belief on the fact that

    A. most depreciation of new cars occurs in the first two to three years.

    B. used cars have better warranties than new cars.

    C. used cars cost less to operate than new cars because they've been broken in.

    D. registration costs more for older cars than newer cars.

36. What is one disadvantage of a travel and entertainment card?

    A. The balance must be paid in full each month.

    B. A person can withhold payment regardless of the amount of the disputed charge.

    C. If the store issuing the card goes bankrupt, the cardholder is out the money he or she spent to buy the card.

    D. If a card is stolen, the person has two days to notify the issuer without penalty.

37. Which of the following may be deducted in calculating personal income taxes?

    A. Health savings account contributions for the fiscal year

    B. Life insurance premiums

    C. Expenses related to moving to assisted living

    D. Support for an elderly parent

38. Which of the following is true about annuities?

    A. They involve a deal between several individuals.

    B. They involve risk because the payouts can be random and unpredictable.

    C. They can be part of a smart retirement planning strategy.

    D. The amount that accumulates each year is taxable each year.

39. When are taxes paid on an estate that was left under a traditional marital share will?

    A. At the time of the death of the spouse whose will is bring probated

    B. At the time of the death of the spouse who survived

    C. No taxes required

    D. Half when the first spouse dies and half when the surviving spouse dies

40. Which of the following is true about equities?

    A. They only involve companies from certain industries that meet minimum revenue thresholds.

    B. They always involve a greater degree of risk than bonds.

    C. Investors hope to profit via a drop in the stock prices.

    D. Doing research by consulting a variety of available sources can greatly increase the odds of financial profits.

41. Which of the following forms does a worker complete to indicate the number of exemptions he or she has for tax purposes?

A. W-2
B. W-4
C. 1040
D. 1099

42. Stan bought a used car with no express warranties. He may still have certain protections under

A. an implied warranty.
B. an extended warranty.
C. federal lemon laws.
D. judicial warranties.

43. Achieving financial goals depends on how

A. much a person earns and saves.
B. much a person earns, saves, and invests.
C. well the stock market performs.
D. well the economy performs.

44. A qualified pension plan is

A. a defined contribution plan.
B. taxable at the time that contributions are made.
C. guaranteed by the Pension Benefit Guaranty Corporation.
D. available only to industries with unions.

45. Which of the following is a retirement plan for self-employed persons?

A. SEP
B. SIMPLE
C. 403(b)
D. Keogh

46. The limit on the amount a monthly mortgage payment may be increased on an adjustable rate mortgage is known as the

A. rate cap.
B. buy-down.
C. payment cap.
D. loan cap.

47. In a no-fault auto insurance plan state, which of the following is typically required?

A. Only property damage insurance

B. Only insurance to cover medical expenses

C. Only insurance to cover damage and medical expenses of the victim(s) of the accident, not the person who caused it

D. Uninsured motorist coverage

48. Paul buys the right to purchase from his broker 100 shares of a stock at $43 a share within thirty days. This is known as

A. selling short.

B. trading in a call option.

C. buying on margin.

D. day trading.

49. Which of the following is NOT included when calculating debt-to-income ratio?

A. Car loan payment

B. Student loan payment

C. Mortgage payment

D. Payments for utilities

50. Which of the following is an example of an open-end credit instrument?

A. A mortgage

B. A three-year vehicle loan

C. A home equity line of credit

D. An installment cash credit

51. A flexible spending account can be used to

A. pay for health care.

B. pay for adult day care for an elderly relative.

C. put aside money to pay estimated taxes.

D. pay for retirement expenses.

52. Which of the following is NOT one of the "five Cs of credit worthiness" considered by creditors?

A. Capacity
B. Cash on hand
C. Capital
D. Conditions

53. Which of the following is a difference between a credit card and a debit card?

A. The bank will certify that a person has sufficient funds to cover a purchase with a debit card but not a credit card.
B. A debit card is preloaded with a certain amount, whereas the credit card can be used up to the credit limit on the card.
C. Losses from a stolen credit card are capped at $500, whereas with a debit card, losses are capped at $50.
D. With a credit card, there is float between the time a person charges a purchase and the person is billed, whereas with a debit card, the amount of the purchase is withdrawn from the account immediately.

54. Which of the following is NOT taxed as part of an estate?

A. Traditional IRA
B. Roth IRA
C. Irrevocable trust
D. Testamentary trust

55. Which of the following is true about income tax?

A. It always involves the federal government.
B. Salary is the only type of income considered.
C. Passive types of income can be taxable.
D. Withholding refers to an amount an individual sets aside in their savings account to pay their tax bill.

56. Reverse mortgages are a good idea for people who

A. are seeking a way to obtain more cash or lower/eliminate some monthly payments.
B. are at least 45 years of age.
C. have no equity in their home.
D. do not own a home.

57. Which of the following investments is the best choice for someone with low risk-tolerance?

A. Individual stocks
B. Bond mutual funds
C. Stock mutual funds
D. Money market funds

58. A will that divides an estate per stirpes divides assets

A. equally among branches of a family.
B. into equal shares for distribution.
C. according to stated amounts in the will.
D. equally between spouse and children.

59. Manjeet invests in a municipal bond fund for its tax benefit. What is the benefit that he derives from this investment?

A. The fund enables him to evade paying taxes.
B. The fund provides him with a tax credit.
C. The interest earned is tax-exempt.
D. The interest earned is tax-deferred.

60. Which of the following regulates investment advisers?

A. State securities regulator
B. Sarbanes-Oxley
C. Certified Financial Planner Board of Standards, Inc.
D. FINRA

ANSWER KEY AND EXPLANATIONS

1. A	13. A	25. A	37. A	49. D
2. B	14. B	26. B	38. C	50. C
3. A	15. A	27. B	39. D	51. A
4. C	16. A	28. A	40. D	52. B
5. A	17. C	29. D	41. B	53. D
6. B	18. A	30. C	42. A	54. C
7. D	19. A	31. A	43. B	55. C
8. C	20. C	32. C	44. C	56. A
9. D	21. B	33. A	45. D	57. D
10. D	22. D	34. B	46. C	58. A
11. B	23. B	35. A	47. B	59. C
12. C	24. C	36. A	48. B	60. A

1. **The correct answer is A.** In the event that a homebuyer has less than 20 percent for a down payment, he or she will need to purchase mortgage insurance. Choice B is incorrect because the FHA doesn't offer mortgages; it insures mortgages. Choice C is incorrect for the same reason. In addition, the VA doesn't require mortgage insurance. Choice D is incorrect because there is no requirement for such a down payment related to mortgage insurance.

2. **The correct answer is B.** CDs are purchased for a specified amount of money at a specified interest rate for a specified period. Choice A is incorrect because the interest rate doesn't vary for CDs, but it does vary over time for savings accounts and money market accounts. Choice C is incorrect because all three are FDIC-insured as long as they are less than $250,000. Choice D is incorrect because all three are good savings vehicles for people with low risk-tolerance.

3. **The correct answer is A.** Future value is the value of an asset or cash at a specific date in the future. Choice B defines time value of money, not future value of money. Choice C misstates the definition of the present value of money: the current value for a future amount of money calculated with a specific interest rate for a specific period of time. Choice D is the definition of a return.

4. The correct answer is C. Vested benefits are those to which an individual is entitled after they resign, regardless of how they terminated their employment or notified the employer. Vesting often does not go into effect until a minimum length of service has been completed (choice A). An employee's rights to vested benefits are protected under the Employee Retirement Income Security Act (choice B), but only certain types of benefits are considered legally protected vested benefits (choice D).

5. The correct answer is A. A person pays taxes on contributions to a Roth IRA, whereas contributions to traditional IRAs (choice B) and spousal IRAs (choice C) are tax-deductible, and the withdrawals are taxed. Contributions to SEPs (choice D) are made with pretax income, but earnings are taxed when withdrawn.

6. The correct answer is B. A Chapter 13 bankruptcy filing remains on a person's credit report for seven years. Five years (choice A) is the number of years in which a person with regular income must pay off debts current at the time of Chapter 13 bankruptcy filing. A person may file for Chapter 7 bankruptcy only once in eight years (choice C), and a record of a Chapter 7 bankruptcy filing remains on a person's credit report for ten years (choice D).

7. The correct answer is D. Jason needs some cash to fall back on in case he loses his job, has an accident, or is sick for a prolonged period. While paying off his student loan (choice A), setting up a retirement plan (choice B), and buying life insurance (choice C) are important, financial planning involves prioritizing needs and setting staged goals. The immediate need is an emergency fund. Second to that, if his new employer offers a retirement plan with employer contributions, then he should consider contributing so that his retirement plan account can collect the "free money" from the employer.

8. The correct answer is C. Tax credits are applied after the income tax is calculated, which is after the standard deductions and any exemptions are taken, not before as choice D erroneously indicates. Choices A and B are actually the same answer and are both incorrect; they are the first step in calculating income tax.

9. **The correct answer is D.** Because of the initial upfront expenses, such as closing costs, purchasing a home may not be worth the initial costs for those who plan to be in the property for a short time. In this case, renting may be wiser. Choices A, B, and C are valid reasons to consider purchasing a home.

10. **The correct answer is D.** Term life pays death benefits only. Choice A describes the benefits offered by a whole life policy. Choices B and C are incomplete benefits of whole life policies.

11. **The correct answer is B.** A decline in property values is a risk of buying any type of home. Association rules (choice A) refers to planned unit developments, condominiums, and co-operatives, not stand-alone homes. Lack of privacy (choice C) may occur in condos and co-ops, but not stand-alone homes. Assessment fees (choice D) again apply to forms of ownership other than stand-alone homes that are not part of planned unit developments.

12. **The correct answer is C.** For the purpose of receiving Social Security, full retirement age for those born between 1943 and 1954 is 66. The age at which people may begin taking partial Social Security is $62\frac{1}{2}$ (choice A). Full retirement age for those born prior to 1943 was 65 (choice B). The age at which those born after 1960 may begin receiving full benefits under Social Security is 67 (choice D).

13. **The correct answer is A.** The opportunity cost of choosing one thing over another is the loss of the benefit of what was not chosen. Choosing one item over another may be a lost opportunity (choice B), but that's not an economic concept, so eliminate it. Alternative (choice C) also is not an economic concept, so eliminate it. Choice D is simply the exchange of one thing for another; there is no value placed on the items, so it doesn't match the definition.

14. **The correct answer is B.** A consumer would most likely take into consideration the features of a refrigerator first. A volume discount (choice A) doesn't make sense because consumers typically buy only one refrigerator at a time. Choice C also wouldn't be relevant since trade-in value generally applies to cars or other large purchases with extended lifespans. A service contract (choice D) is usually not a good buy for consumers because products tend to fail within the first year when they are still under warranty.

15. **The correct answer is A.** Liquidity refers to the ability to quickly access money or turn an asset into cash. Choice B is incorrect because, in general, liquid assets involve low interest rates and aren't considered highly profitable in the short term. Choice C is incorrect because accounts that require a lot of bureaucratic back-and-forth or time-consuming paperwork to adjust or cash out wouldn't usually be considered desirable as a liquid asset. Choice D is incorrect because assets or accounts that cannot be touched for a long period of time aren't considered highly liquid.

16. **The correct answer is A.** When a person needs cash, a regular checking account is the fastest way to get it—whether by ATM or check. There is no penalty involved—assuming there is no overdraft. Choices B and C are incorrect because there is a penalty for early withdrawal of both CDs and Series EE bonds. The former is typically a month's interest, and the latter is three months' interest. A person may be able to sell stocks (choice D) quickly, assuming it's a day when the stock market is open, but there could be a "penalty" if the stock is sold below the price the person paid for it.

17. **The correct answer is C.** Although checking a credit score (choice D) is important to ensure that it is accurate, it won't help that credit score if a person doesn't use credit wisely. Opening a savings account and making regular deposits provides a way to show that a person can be disciplined when it comes to money. Overusing credit doesn't demonstrate that; both choices A and B can send up red flags to potential creditors. The more inquiries for new credit that show up, the less responsible the person seems.

18. The correct answer is A. Social Security taxes, known as FICA (Federal Insurance Contributions Act) consist of Medicare and Old Age Survivors Benefit and are automatically taken out of an employee's paycheck. Pension plans, such as 401(k) and 403(b) plans (choice B), and insurance coverage, such as long-term care insurance (choice C) and health insurance (choice D), are all voluntary nontax payroll deductions.

19. The correct answer is A. Health maintenance organizations (HMOs) are both insurers and care providers. A preferred provider organization (choice B) is a provider, not an insurer, as is a point of service plan (choice C). Choice D is known as fee-for-service health insurance (FFS) and is an insurer only.

20. The correct answer is C. The cost-of-living protection is a rider that is typically added to a life insurance policy because of the effects of inflation in the long term. The grace period (choice A), the automatic premium clause (choice B), and the policy loan provision (choice D) are common parts of a life insurance policy. The first provides a window to pay the premium on a policy without incurring a penalty; the second enables the insurance company to pay the premium from the cash value of the policy should the policyholder not pay the premium within the grace period; and the third enables the policyholder to borrow against the cash value of the policy.

21. The correct answer is B. The card was not a good choice because it charged interest from the day that a purchase was made. A 21-day grace period (choice A) and buyer purchase protection (choice C) would be reasons for, not against, taking the card. While a waived annual fee (choice D) might be beneficial for the time period specified in the special offer, it might not be a good deal in the long term if an annual fee is reinstated after the first year.

22. **The correct answer is D.** Reduction of the principal borrowed over the life of a loan is called amortization. RESPA (choice A) stands for Real Estate Settlement Procedures Act and refers to closing costs and the closing process for buying a home. A rate cap (choice B) is the amount by which the interest rate can increase or decrease over the life of an adjustable rate mortgage. Don't be tripped up by the word escrow in choice C. This answer is incorrect because an escrow account holds money to pay property taxes and sometimes homeowner's insurance. The lender sets up the account and deposits part of each month's mortgage payment from the homeowner into the account.

23. **The correct answer is B.** FICA payroll deductions are the Social Security and Medicare contributions that workers make. Choice A is incorrect because some payroll deductions are voluntary. Choice C confuses IRAs with 401(k) and 403(b) pension plans; deductions for the last two are taken, but contributions to IRAs are not. Choice D is incorrect; an employee can opt into a company-sponsored life insurance program and have the premium deducted, but this is not true for a non-company–sponsored policy.

24. **The correct answer is C.** COBRA stands for the Consolidated Omnibus Budget Reconciliation Act of 1986. Under this law, many employers are required to offer terminated and laid-off workers the opportunity to continue their health insurance under the employer's plan. HIPAA (choice A) stands for Health Insurance Portability and Accountability Act of 1996, which ensures that workers cannot be required to requalify for health insurance when they change jobs or be charged more for health insurance than current employees. Medigap (choice B) refers to supplemental health insurance for people covered under Medicare. COB (choice D) stands for coordination of benefits, a provision of health insurance policies that enables a policyholder to receive reimbursement from several health insurance policies up to 100 percent of allowable medical costs that the person paid.

25. **The correct answer is A.** A current liability is one that must be paid within a year. A noncurrent liability (choice B) is one that does not have to be paid within a year. Flexible expense (choice C) refers to an expense that is controllable; that is, a person can choose to take on the expense or not. Dissavings (choice D) occurs when a person's expenses are greater than his or her income, resulting in a decrease in net worth.

26. **The correct answer is B.** Comparing prices and deals among various retailers—which can be done quickly and easily online—helps ensure you are getting the best deal. Buying with credit (choice A) means you may incur interest charges (although you may be able to avoid this if you pay off the balance within the grace period or use a card that offers a no-interest introductory rate). Withdrawing money from savings, CDs, or other accounts (choice C) means losing out on potential future interest earnings. In general, optional service plans (choice D) don't tend to offer a good return on investment.

27. **The correct answer is B.** A person may withdraw money from a traditional IRA for three reasons, namely, to pay large medical expenses, for higher education, or for a first home.

28. **The correct answer is A.** Indemnity insurance limits payments to a specified amount regardless of actual costs; expense insurance is a better deal. Choice B is incorrect because the type of indemnity insurance may or may not cover pre-existing conditions; that is not why it is indemnity insurance. Choice C is incorrect because indemnity insurance pays the patient directly, not the healthcare provider. Choice D describes physicians' expense insurance.

29. **The correct answer is D.** An umbrella policy adds liability coverage over and above regular homeowner's and auto insurance policies. Choice A is incorrect because an umbrella policy would only cover a home office if the underlying homeowner's policy had an endorsement covering it. Choice B is incorrect because flood insurance is a separate policy. Choice C is incorrect because an umbrella policy doesn't include health insurance, and it doesn't provide homeowner's and auto insurance as such, but increases liability coverage.

30. **The correct answer is C.** Because this structure doesn't increase with one's income or ability to pay, a lower-income person will end up paying a larger portion of their income than someone who is wealthier, if they are both charged the same amount. Since this type of tax often includes a flat fee or standard percentage rate, it is fairly easy to calculate, not complicated as choice A indicates. Choice B is incorrect because people aren't negatively impacted by moving to a higher tax bracket. The opposite of choice D is true. Regressive income can offer motivation to earn more, as an individual will have more disposable income since the tax rate will not increase.

31. **The correct answer is A.** Smart asset allocation involves developing a strategy that helps achieve long-term goals with a level of risk deemed tolerable. Choice B is incorrect because there is no one-size-fits-all standard formula; asset allocation is an individual decision determined by specific financial circumstances and objectives. Choice C is too strict; the details of an asset allocation plan will likely change regularly as needs and goals dictate. Choice D refers to dividing investments into specific categories, not physically separating them and giving them away.

32. **The correct answer is C.** Estimated tax payments are due quarterly: April 15, June 15, September 15, and the following January 15.

33. The correct answer is A. Mutual funds involve stock in a variety of companies, so a portfolio is diversified and there is less risk since the portfolio isn't depending on the performance of one individual company. Choice B is incorrect because, like other types of stocks, mutual funds aren't federally insured. The opposite of choice C is true. The profit or loss can fluctuate and may be unpredictable. Choice D is incorrect because the investor does not make the selection; the amount invested is spread across a mixture of companies.

34. The correct answer is B. Moody's Investors Services is a bond credit-rating organization that also provides research and analysis related to investments. It rates bonds depending on the strength and credit worthiness of the company behind them, but doesn't provide credit repair services to businesses (choice A). It also doesn't set prices for stock or bonds, whose prices can go up and down depending on a range of factors (choice C). This company also doesn't provide accounting service or serve as a personal financial adviser (choice D).

35. The correct answer is A. New cars depreciate more rapidly than older cars, so buying a used car can make financial sense. Choice B is incorrect; many used cars come with no express warranties. Choice C is incorrect because the older a car is, the more maintenance is typically required. Choice D is incorrect because registration typically costs less, not more, in most states.

36. The correct answer is A. The balance on travel and entertainment (T&E) cards must be paid in full each month. Choice B is incorrect because a person can withhold payment on a T&E card only if the amount is over $50. Choice C describes a store gift card. Choice D is incorrect because a person is still liable for charges under $50 regardless of the type of charge card.

37. The correct answer is A. Contributions to a health savings account (HSA) are tax deductible up to certain IRS limits. Life insurance premiums (choice B), expenses related to moving to assisted living (choice C), and support for an elderly parent (choice D) are not deductible.

38. **The correct answer is C.** Because an investor can anticipate a specific payout at some future point (either in a lump sum or yearly increments), this can be a great retirement planning tool. Choice A is incorrect because an annuity involves an agreement between an individual and a company. The payout of an annuity is always fixed and predetermined, which makes choice B incorrect. Choice D is incorrect because money that accumulates is tax-deferred.

39. **The correct answer is D.** Under a traditional marital share will, half the taxes are paid when the first spouse dies and half when the surviving spouse dies. Choice A describes tax payment under a simple will.

40. **The correct answer is D.** There are a wide range of resources available to help you become a smart investor in equities, including corporate reports and financial news programs. Choice A is incorrect because equities can involve a range of companies of all sizes from many industries. Choice B is incorrect because equities don't necessarily have a greater or lesser degree of risk than bonds—it depends on the quality of the bonds the investor buys. The opposite of choice C is true. An investor would hope to profit via capital gains realized when the stock rises.

41. **The correct answer is B.** The W-4 lists exemptions. The W-2 (choice A) is an employer's form listing an employee's income for the year. A 1040 (choice C) is the income tax long form. A 1099 (choice D) is the form that self-employed people receive from companies that employed them during the year.

42. **The correct answer is A.** Even if a used car dealership doesn't specifically mention a warranty, there are certain warranty protections that may be assumed unless otherwise stated. This would not be the case if the car is sold "as is," although certain states have laws that prohibit dealers from selling "as is" cars with no warranties. An extended warranty (choice B) is often the term used for a service contract that "extends" the protection of express warranties. Federal lemon laws (choice C) only apply to the purchase of new vehicles, although a handful of states do have some type of lemon laws for purchases involving used cars. Choice D doesn't exist.

43. The correct answer is B. While it is true that a person will probably do better in a good economy (choice D) or if the stock market
performs well (choice C)—assuming the person owns stocks or
shares in stock funds—the major factors are how much a person
earns, saves, and invests. Choice A is incorrect because it omits
the concept of investing.

44. The correct answer is C. A qualified pension plan is one that
meets all the requirements under the Employee Retirement
Income Security Act of 1974 (ERISA) and is guaranteed by the
Pension Benefit Guaranty Corporation. Choice A is incorrect
because it is only part of what is true about qualified pension
plans; a qualified pension plan may be a defined contribution or
a defined benefit plan. Choice B is incorrect because in terms of
taxation, whether a plan is qualified or not is irrelevant. Taxes
are paid at the time that contributions are made if the plan is a
Roth IRA, not if it is a 401(k). Taxes on the latter are paid when
withdrawals are made. Choice D is incorrect because a qualified
pension plan is open to any company in any industry.

45. The correct answer is D. Keoghs, also known as HR-10 plans,
are retirement plans for self-employed persons. A SEP or Simple
Employee Pension Plan (choice A) is set up by an employer. A
SIMPLE or Savings Incentive Match Plans for Employees (choice
B) was created for small employers to use. A 403(b) plan (choice
C) is an employer-sponsored pension plan for nonprofits, similar
to 401(k) plans for for-profit companies.

46. The correct answer is C. The payment cap limits how much
a monthly payment on an adjustable rate mortgage may be
increased. An annual rate cap (choice A) limits the amount
that an interest rate may increase, and it may also put a floor on
how far a rate may decrease. A buy-down (choice B) is a form
of financing that builders of a newly constructed house offer to
buyers. The term *loan cap* (choice D) is too general.

47. **The correct answer is B.** Personal injury protection (PIP) insurance is required in no-fault insurance states to cover medical expenses and accident-related expenses such as loss of income. No-fault insurance policies typically don't cover damage to property (choice A); therefore, buying insurance to cover property damage in the event of an accident is important. Choice C is incorrect for two reasons: (1) property insurance is not required, and (2) PIP covers the policyholder regardless of whether he or she caused the accident. Uninsured motorist coverage (choice D) is not required under a no-fault insurance system.

48. **The correct answer is B.** A call option is based on the assumption or wish that the stock will rise in value and the investor will make money on it. Selling short (choice A) occurs when an investor borrows stock from a broker with the intention of selling it at a higher price and then buying it back when the value decreases, thus making money on the difference between the price sold on the borrowed stock and the price paid to replace the stock. Buying on margin (choice C) is buying stock in part with borrowed money. Day trading (choice D) is a method of buying and selling stocks constantly rather than holding them for any period of time.

49. **The correct answer is D.** In calculating the debt-to-income ratio, payments for debts and other liabilities are factored into the equation, so that would include a car loan (choice A), a student loan (choice B), and the mortgage payment (choice C). Costs for utilities, maintenance, and other household expenses are not considered.

50. **The correct answer is C.** A home equity line of credit is an open-end credit instrument because it enables a consumer to make a series of purchases over a period of time, as long as the consumer doesn't go over the amount of the line of credit. The consumer must repay the amount in regular payments, but the payments may be of varying amounts. Choices A, B, and D are all examples of closed-end credit, used for a specific purchase for a specific period and for a specific amount of money.

51. The correct answer is A. A flexible spending account can be used to pay for qualified health care, medical supplies, and child care. Choice B is not an approved use of flexible spending funds, nor are estimated taxes (choice C) and retirement expenses (choice D).

52. The correct answer is B. The amount of cash on hand can of course impact the ability to pay bills, but creditors have no way of monitoring or tracking that. However, they do evaluate the ability to take on more debt (choice A), net worth (choice C), and outside factors that may impact a financial situation (choice D).

53. The correct answer is D. A person using a credit card has time between charging a purchase and when the money for it is due, unlike a person using a debit card, which immediately subtracts the purchase price from the user's bank account. Choice A confuses a certified check with a debit card. Choice B confuses a smart card with a debit card; smart cards are preloaded with an amount. Neither a debit card nor a credit card is preloaded. Choice C is inaccurate; losses from a stolen credit card are capped at $50, but losses from a stolen debit card are capped at $50 only if the person notifies the bank in fewer than two days. If it's between two and sixty days before the bank is notified, losses are capped at $500.

54. The correct answer is C. An irrevocable trust is not part of an estate for probate and estate taxation purposes. Traditional and Roth IRAs and testamentary trusts (choices A, B, and D), which are trusts set up by a will, are subject to probate and estate taxes.

55. The correct answer is C. Passive income can refer to amounts received from things like royalties, partnerships, or ongoing pay-outs. Choice A is only partially correct because income tax can also be owed to state or local governments. Choice B is incorrect because a taxpayer may owe taxes on other types of wages, in addition to self-employment, business profits, and other sources of income. Choice D is incorrect because withholding refers to the amount an employer takes out of the employee's paycheck each pay period for income taxes.

56. **The correct answer is A.** Reverse mortgages allow homeowners to "cash out" on some of their home's equity, without owing any monthly payments. The other choices are inaccurate. In order to qualify, they must be at least age 62 and have some equity in a property they own.

57. **The correct answer is D.** Money market funds are sold by securities brokers for $1 per share, and, even though the funds are not FDIC insured, they are principal protected, so the value of a share does not drop below a dollar. Individual stocks, bond mutual funds, and stock mutual funds (choices A, B, and C) are not good choices for individuals with low risk-tolerance because they are not insured or principal protected, which means they can lose value.

58. **The correct answer is A.** *Per stirpes* means that assets are divided equally among the branches of a family. Choice B describes a per capita distribution. Choice C refers to a stated dollar amount will. Choice D is incorrect because per stirpes includes the extended family, not just the immediate family.

59. **The correct answer is C.** The interest earned on municipal bonds is tax-exempt. Choice A is incorrect because Manjeet is avoiding paying taxes, which is legal; he is not evading taxes, which is illegal. Choice B is incorrect because a tax credit is deducted directly from taxable income and has nothing to do with municipal bonds. Choice D is incorrect because he will not have to pay taxes later.

60. **The correct answer is A.** Investment advisers may be regulated by their state's securities regulator or by the SEC, depending on the size of the assets the person manages. Sarbanes-Oxley (choice B) regulates the financial disclosure of corporations. The Certified Financial Planner Board of Standards, Inc. (choice C) licenses financial planners, which is different from an investment adviser. FINRA (choice D) is a self-policing association of securities firms.